David Sang

Cambridge IGCSE®
Physical Science

Physics Workbook

CAMBRIDGE
UNIVERSITY PRESS

University Printing House, Cambridge CB2 8BS, United Kingdom

One Liberty Plaza, 20th Floor, New York, NY 10006, USA

477 Williamstown Road, Port Melbourne, VIC 3207, Australia

4843/24, 2nd Floor, Ansari Road, Daryaganj, Delhi – 110002, India

79 Anson Road, #06–04/06, Singapore 079906

Cambridge University Press is part of the University of Cambridge.

It furthers the University's mission by disseminating knowledge in the pursuit of education, learning and research at the highest international levels of excellence.

www.cambridge.org
Information on this title: www.cambridge.org/9781316633526

© Cambridge University Press 2017

First published 2017
20 19 18 17 16 15 14 13 12 11 10 9 8 7 6 5 4 3 2

Printed in Spain by GraphyCems

A catalogue record for this publication is available from the British Library

ISBN 978-1-316-63352-6 Paperback

Introduction   v

P1 Making measurements   1

P1.1 The SI system of units   1

P1.2 Paper measurements   2

P1.3 Density data   3

P1.4 Density of steel   5

P1.5 Testing your body clock   6

P2 Describing motion   8

P2.1 Measuring speed   8

P2.2 Speed calculations   11

P2.3 More speed calculations   12

P2.4 Distance–time graphs   14

P2.5 Acceleration   18

P2.6 Velocity–time graphs   19

P3 Forces and motion   22

P3.1 Identifying forces   22

P3.2 The effects of forces   23

P3.3 Combining forces   24

P3.4 Force, mass and acceleration   25

P3.5 Mass and weight   27

P3.6 Falling   28

P4 Turning effects of forces   30

P4.1 Turning effect of a force   30

P4.2 Calculating moments   31

P4.3 Stability and centre of mass   33

P4.4 Finding the centre of mass of a thin
      sheet of card   34

P4.5 Make a mobile   35

P5 Forces and matter   37

P5.1 Stretching a spring   37

P5.2 Stretching rubber   39

P5.3 Pressure   40

**P6 Energy transformations and
      energy transfers   43**

P6.1 Recognising forms of energy   43

P6.2 Energy efficiency   45

P6.3 Energy calculations   47

P7 Energy resources   51

P7.1 Renewables and non-renewables   51

P7.2 Wind energy   53

P7.3 Energy from the Sun   55

P8 Work and power   56

P8.1 Forces doing work, transferring energy   56

P8.2 Calculating work done   58

P8.3 Measuring work done   60

P8.4 Power   61

P9 The kinetic model of matter   63

P9.1 Changes of state   63

P9.2 The kinetic model of matter   65

P9.3 Understanding gases   66

P10 Thermal properties of matter   67

P10.1 Calibrating a thermometer   67

P10.2 Practical thermometers   69

P10.3 Demonstrating thermal expansion   70

P10.4 Thermal expansion   71

P11 Thermal (heat) energy transfers   73

P11.1 Conductors of heat   73

P11.2 Convection currents   74

P11.3 Radiation   76

P11.4 Losing heat   78

P11.5 Absorb, emit, reflect   79

P12 Sound   81

P12.1 Sound on the move   81

P12.2 Sound as a wave   84

iii

P13 Light   **86**

P13.1 On reflection   87

P13.2 Refraction of light   88

P13.3 The changing speed of light   89

P13.4 A perfect mirror   90

P13.5 Image in a lens   92

P14 Properties of waves   **94**

P14.1 Describing waves   94

P14.2 The speed of waves   96

P14.3 Wave phenomena   97

P15 Spectra   **99**

P15.1 Electromagnetic waves   99

P15.2 Using electromagnetic radiation   100

P16 Magnetism   **102**

P16.1 Attraction and repulsion   102

P16.2 Make a magnet   103

P16.3 Magnetising, demagnetising   104

P16.4 Magnetic fields   105

P17 Static electricity   **106**

P17.1 Attraction and repulsion   106

P17.2 Static at home   108

P18 Electrical quantities   **109**

P18.1 Current in a circuit   110

P18.2 Voltage in electric circuits   111

P18.3 Current and charge   112

P18.4 Electrical resistance   113

P18.5 Electrical energy and power   115

P19 Electric circuits   **117**

P19.1 Circuit components and
       their symbols   117

P19.2 Resistor combinations   118

P19.3 More resistor combinations   120

P19.4 Resistance of a wire   122

P19.5 Electrical safety   124

P20 Electromagnetism   **126**

P20.1 Using electromagnetism   126

P20.2 Electricity generation   127

P20.3 Transformers   128

P21 The nuclear atom   **131**

P21.1 The structure of the atom   131

P21.2 Isotopes   133

P22 Radioactivity   **134**

P22.1 The nature of radiation   134

P22.2 Radioactive decay
       equations   136

P22.3 Radioactive decay   137

Answers   **141**

This workbook contains exercises designed to help you develop the skills needed for success in Cambridge IGCSE® Physical Science.

The examination tests three different Assessment Objectives, or AOs for short. These are:

AO1 Knowledge with understanding

AO2 Handling information and problem solving

AO3 Experimental skills and investigations.

In the examination, about 50% of the marks are for AO1, 30% for AO2 and 20% for AO3. Just learning your work and remembering it is therefore not enough to make sure that you get the best possible grade in the exam. Half of all the marks are for AO2 and AO3. You need to be able to use what you've learnt in unfamiliar contexts (AO2) and to demonstrate your experimental skills (AO3).

This workbook contains exercises to help you to develop AO2 and AO3 further. There are some questions that just involve remembering things you have been taught (AO1), but most of the questions require you to use what you've learnt to work out, for example, what a set of data means, or to suggest how an experiment might be improved.

These exercises are not intended to be exactly like the questions you will get on your exam papers. This is because they are meant to help you to develop your skills, rather than testing you on them.

There's an introduction at the start of each exercise that tells you the purpose of it – which skills you will be working with as you answer the questions.

The exercises cover both Core and Supplement material of the syllabus. The Supplement material can be identified by the Supplement bar in the margin (as shown). This indicates that the exercise is intended for students who are studying the Supplement content of the syllabus as well as the Core.

Safety

A few practical exercises have been included. These could be carried out at home using simple materials that you are likely to have available to you. (There are many more practical activities on the CD-ROM that accompanies your textbook.)

While carrying out such experiments, it is your responsibility to think about your own safety, and the safety of others. If you work sensibly and assess any risks before starting, you should come to no harm. If you are in doubt, discuss what you are going to do with your teacher before you start.

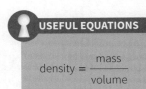

A DEFINITION TO LEARN

density: the mass per unit volume

USEFUL EQUATIONS

$$\text{density} = \frac{\text{mass}}{\text{volume}}$$

Exercise P1.1 The SI system of units

> To be part of the international community of scientists, you need to use the SI units (Le Système International d'Unités).

a Give the SI units (name and symbol) of the following quantities:

length

....

volume

....

b Give the name in words and the symbol for the following:

one thousand metres

....

one-thousandth of a metre

....

c How many

centimetres are there in a metre?   ....

dm³ are there in a cubic metre?   ....

d List as many non-SI units of length as you can.

....

....

e Give a reason why it is important for scientists to have a system of units that is agreed between all countries.

....

....

f Name some more professions that make use of the SI system of units.

....

....

Exercise P1.2 Paper measurements

> **This exercise will test your ability to measure lengths.**

Find a rectangular sheet of paper, at least as big as the pages of this book. A sheet of newspaper is ideal.

Your task is to use a ruler to measure three lengths: the short side, the long side and the diagonal.

For lengths that are longer than your ruler, you will need to devise a careful technique.

a Describe the method you have used for measuring the length of the diagonal. It may help to include a diagram.

....

....

....

....

b Record your results (in centimetres) in the table.

Measurement	Length / cm	Length^2 / cm^2
short side	....	
long side	....	
diagonal	....	

c Now you can use Pythagoras' theorem to test your results. In the third column of the table, calculate and write down the square of each length.

Then calculate:

(short side)^2 + (long side)^2 = ...

This should be equal to (diagonal)^2.

Round off your values to the nearest cm^2.

d How close are your two answers? Write a comment below.

....

....

....

Exercise P1.3 Density data

> This exercise presents some data for you to interpret and use.

Some data about the density of various solids and liquids are shown in the table.

Material	State / type	Density / kg/m^3	Density / g/cm^3
water	liquid / non-metal	1000	1.000
ethanol	liquid / non-metal	800	0.800
olive oil	liquid / non-metal	920	
mercury	liquid / metal	13 500	
ice	solid / non-metal	920	
diamond	solid / non-metal	3500	
cork	solid / non-metal	250	
chalk	solid / non-metal	2700	
iron	solid / metal	7900	
tungsten	solid / metal	19 300	
aluminium	solid / metal	2700	
gold	solid / metal	19 300	

Two units are used for the densities, kg/m^3 and g/cm^3.

a Complete the second column by converting each density in kg/m^3 to the equivalent value in g/cm^3. The first two have been done for you.

b Use the data to explain why ice floats on water.

....

....

c A cook mixes equal volumes of water and olive oil in a jar. The two liquids separate. Complete the drawing of the jar to show how the liquids will appear. Label them.

d A student wrote: "These data show that metals are denser than non-metals." Do you agree? Explain your answer.

....

....

....

....

e Calculate the mass of a block of gold that measures 20 cm × 15 cm × 10 cm. Give your answer in kg.

f A metalworker finds a block of silvery metal. He weighs it and he measures its volume. Here are his results:

mass of block = 0.270 kg

volume of block = 14.0 cm³

Calculate the density of the block.

Suggest what metal this might be ....

Exercise P1.4 Density of steel

In this exercise, you can explain how to find the density of an irregularly-shaped object.

a A student has to determine the density of steel. Her teacher gives her several steel bolts.

The student half-fills a measuring cylinder with water. She then submerges several of the steel bolts in the water.

What quantities should she record in order to find the volume of the bolts?

....

....

b How can she calculate the volume of the bolts?

....

c State one precaution that she should take in determining the volume of the bolts.

....

....

....

d In order to determine the density of steel, she must also find the mass of the bolts. What instrument should she use for this?

....

e State one precaution that she should take in determining the mass of the bolts.

....

....

....

Exercise P1.5 Testing your body clock

> **How good would your pulse be as a means of measuring time intervals?**

Galileo used the regular pulse of his heart as a means of measuring intervals of time until he noticed that a swinging pendulum was more reliable.

In this exercise, you need to be able to measure the pulse in your wrist. Place two fingers of one hand gently on the inside of the opposite wrist. Press gently at different points until you find the pulse. (Alternatively, press two fingers gently under your jawbone on either side of your neck.)

You will also need a clock or watch that will allow you to measure intervals of time in seconds.

a Start by timing 10 pulses. (Remember to start counting from zero: 0, 1, 2, 3, …, 9, 10.) Repeat this several times and record your results in the table below.

b Comment on your results. How much do they vary? Is the problem that it is difficult to time them, or is your heart rate varying?

....

....

....

c Use your results to calculate the average time for one pulse.

d Repeat the above, but now count 50 pulses. Record your results in the table below. Calculate the average time for one pulse.

e Now investigate how your pulse changes if you take some gentle exercise – for example, by walking briskly, or by walking up and down stairs.

Write up your investigation in the lined space. Use the following as a guide.

- Briefly describe your gentle exercise.

- Give the measurements of pulse rate that you have made.

- Comment on whether you agree with Galileo that a pendulum is a better time-measuring instrument than your pulse.

....

....

....

....

....

....

....

....

....

....

....

....

....

Exercise P2.1 Measuring speed

This exercise is about how we can measure the speed of a moving object.

a One way to find the speed of an object is to measure the time it takes to travel a measured distance. The table shows the three quantities involved.

Complete the table as follows:

- In the second column, give the SI unit for each quantity (name and symbol).

- In the third column, give some other, non-SI, units for these quantities.

- In the fourth column, name suitable measuring instruments for distance and time.

Quantity	SI unit (name and symbol)	Non-SI units	Measuring instrument
distance			
time			
speed			

b In the laboratory, the speed of a moving trolley can be found using two light gates. A timer measures the time taken for a trolley to travel from one light gate to the other.

What other quantity must be measured to determine the trolley's speed?

....

Write down the equation used to calculate the speed of the trolley:

A trolley takes 0.80 s to travel between two light gates, which are separated by 2.24 m. Calculate its average speed.

9

c The speed of moving vehicles is sometimes measured using detectors buried in the road. The two detectors are about 1 m apart. As a vehicle passes over the first detector, an electronic timer starts. As it passes over the second detector, the timer stops.

Explain how the vehicle's speed can then be calculated.

....

....

....

On one stretch of road, any vehicle travelling faster than 25 m/s is breaking the speed limit. The detectors are placed 1.2 m apart. Calculate the speed of a car that takes 0.050 s to travel this distance. Is it breaking the speed limit?

Calculate the shortest time that a car can take to cross the detectors if it is not to break the speed limit.

d Describe briefly how such a speed-detection system could be used to light up a warning light whenever a speeding car goes past.

....

....

....

....

....

Exercise P2.2 Speed calculations

Use the equation for speed to solve some numerical problems.

a   The table shows the time taken for each of three cars to travel 100 m. Circle the name of the fastest car. Complete the table by calculating the speed of each car. Give your answers in m/s and to one decimal place.

Car	Time taken / s	Speed / m/s
red car	4.2	
green car	3.8	
yellow car	4.7	

b   A jet aircraft travels 1200 km in 1 h 20 min.

How many metres does it travel? ....

For how many minutes does it travel? ....

And for how many seconds? ....

Calculate its average speed during its flight.

c   A stone falls 20 m in 2.0 s. Calculate its average speed as it falls.

The stone falls a further 25 m in the next 1.0 s of its fall. Calculate the stone's average speed during the 3 s of its fall.

Explain why we can only calculate the stone's **average** speed during its fall.

....

....

....

Exercise P2.3 More speed calculations

In these problems, you will have to rearrange the equation for speed.

a A car is moving at 22 m/s. How far will it travel in 35 s?

b A swallow can fly at 25 m/s. How long will it take to fly 1.0 km?

c A high-speed train is 180 m long and is travelling at 50 m/s. How long will it take to pass a person standing at a level crossing?

How long will it take to pass completely through a station whose platforms are 220 m in length?

d In a 100 m race, the winner crosses the finishing line in 10.00 s. The runner-up takes 10.20 s. Estimate the distance between the winner and the runner-up as the winner crosses the line. Show your method of working.

Explain why your answer can only be an estimate.

....

....

....

Exercise P2.4 Distance–time graphs

> In this exercise, you draw and interpret some distance–time graphs. You can calculate the speed of an object from the gradient (slope) of the graph.

a The diagrams A–D show distance–time graphs for four moving objects. Complete the table by indicating (in the second column) the graph or graphs that represent the motion described in the first column.

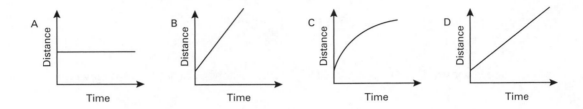

Description of motion	Graph(s)
moving at a steady speed	
stationary (not moving)	
moving fastest	
changing speed	

b The table shows the distance travelled by a runner during a 100 m race. Use the data to draw a distance–time graph on the graph paper grid below.

Distance / m	0	10.0	25.0	45.0	65.0	85.0	105.0
Time / s	0.0	2.0	4.0	6.0	8.0	10.0	12.0

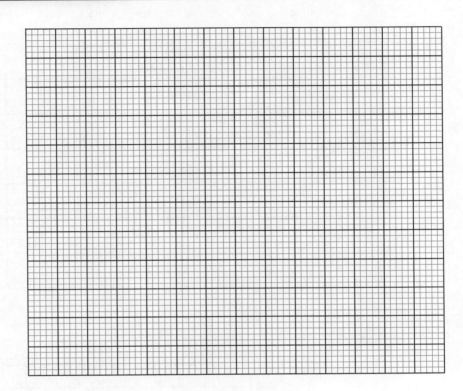

Now use your graph to answer these questions:

How far did the runner travel in the first 9.0 s? ....

How long did the runner take to run the first 50.0 m? ....

How long did the runner take to complete the 100 m? ....

Use the gradient of your graph to determine the runner's average speed between 4.0 s and 10.0 s. On your graph, show the triangle that you use.

c On the graph paper grid below, sketch a distance–time graph for the car whose journey is described here:

- The car set off at a slow, steady speed for 20 s.

- Then it moved for 40 s at a faster speed.

- Then it stopped at traffic lights for 20 s before setting off again at a slow, steady speed.

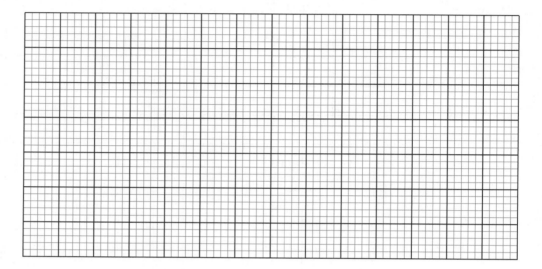

d The graph represents the motion of a bus for part of a journey.

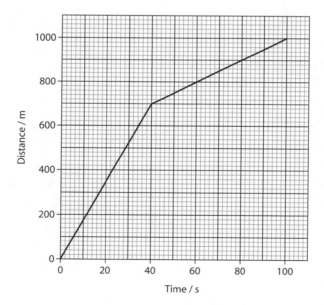

On the graph, mark the section of the journey where the bus was moving faster.

From the graph, calculate the following:

- the speed of the bus when it was moving faster

- the average speed of the bus.

Exercise P2.5 Acceleration

> When an object changes velocity, we say that it accelerates. Its acceleration is the rate at which its velocity increases.

a A car is travelling at 14 m/s. This tells us its *speed*. What further information is required to tell us its *velocity*?

....

b In an advertisement, a car is described like this:

"It can accelerate from 0 km/h to 80 km/h in 10 s."

By how much does its velocity increase in each second (on average)? ....

c A cyclist is travelling at 4.0 m/s. She speeds up to 16 m/s in a time of 5.6 s. Calculate her acceleration.

d A stone falls with an acceleration of 10.0 m/s². Calculate its velocity after falling for 3.5 s.

e On the Moon, gravity is weaker than on Earth. A stone falls with an acceleration of 1.6 m/s². How long will it take to reach a velocity of 10 m/s?

Exercise P2.6 Velocity–time graphs

In this exercise, you draw and interpret some velocity–time graphs. You can calculate the acceleration of an object from the gradient (slope) of the graph. You can calculate the distance travelled from the area under the graph.

a   The diagrams A–D show velocity–time graphs for four moving objects. Complete the table by indicating (in the second column) the graph or graphs that represent the motion described in the first column.

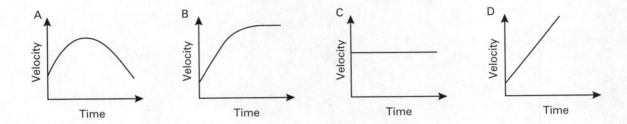

Description of motion	Graph(s)
moving at a constant velocity	
speeding up, then slowing down	
moving with constant acceleration	
accelerating to a constant velocity	

b   The graph represents the motion of a car that accelerates from rest and then travels at a constant velocity.

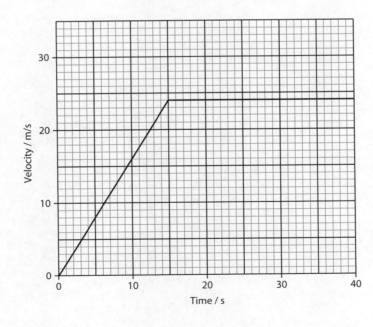

From the graph, determine the acceleration of the car in the first part of its journey.

On the graph, shade in the area that represents the distance travelled by the car while accelerating. Label this area A.

Shade the area that represents the distance travelled by the car at a constant velocity. Label this area B.

Calculate each of these distances and the total distance travelled by the car.

[Note: area of a triangle = $\frac{1}{2}$ × base × height.]

c   On the graph paper grid, sketch a velocity–time graph for the car whose journey is described here:

- The car set off at a slow, constant velocity for 20 s.

- Then, during a time of 10 s, it accelerated to a faster velocity.

- It travelled at this constant velocity for 20 s.

- Then it rapidly decelerated and came to a halt after 10 s.

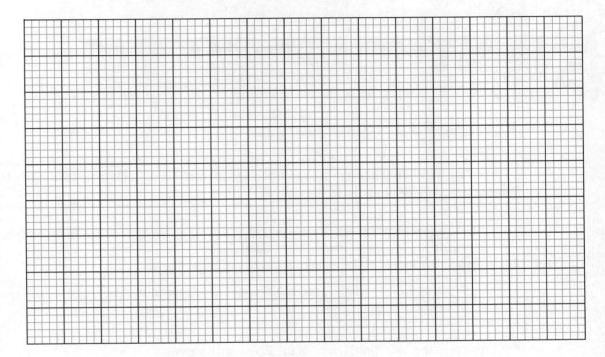

Exercise P3.1 Identifying forces

> Forces are invisible (although we can often see their effects). Being able to identify forces is an important skill for physicists.

The pictures show some bodies. Your task is to add at least one force arrow to each body, showing a force acting on it. (Two force arrows are already shown.)
Each force arrow should be labelled to indicate the following:

1 the type of force (contact, drag/air resistance, weight/gravitational, push/pull, friction, magnetic)
2 the body causing the force
3 the body acted on by the force.

For example: the gravitational force of the Earth on the apple.

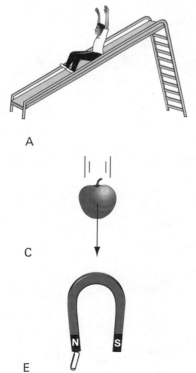

A

B

C

D

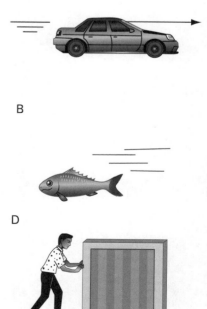

E

F

Exercise P3.2 The effects of forces

> **A force can change how a body moves, or it may change its shape.**

a Each diagram shows a body with a single force acting on it. For each, say what effect the force will have.

A ....

B ....

C ....

D ....

b A boy slides down a sloping ramp. In the space below, draw a diagram of the boy on the ramp and add a labelled arrow to show the force of friction that acts on him.

What effect will the force have on the boy's movement?

....

....

Exercise P3.3 Combining forces

When two or more forces act on a body, we can replace them by a single resultant force that has the same effect.

a   In the table below, the left-hand column shows four objects acted on by different forces. For the same objects in the right-hand column, add a force arrow to show the resultant force acting on it in each case.

Forces on object	Resultant force
80 N →☐← 45 N	☐
60 N →☐← 40 N (50 N ←)	☐
↑20 N 20 N →☐← 20 N ↓40 N	☐
20 N↑ ↑40 N 100 N →☐← 100 N ↓100 N	☐

b   In the space below, draw a diagram showing a body with four forces acting on it. Their resultant force must be 4 N acting vertically downwards.

Exercise P3.4 Force, mass and acceleration

> Here you practise using the relationship $F = ma$.

a The equation $F = ma$ relates three quantities. Complete the table to show the names of these quantities and their SI units.

Quantity	Symbol	SI unit
	F	
	m	
	a	

b Rearrange the equation $F = ma$ to change its subject:

$m =$ $a =$

c Calculate the force needed to give a mass of 20 kg an acceleration of 0.72 m/s^2.

d A car of mass 450 kg is acted on by a resultant force of 1575 N. Calculate its acceleration.

e One way to find the mass of an object is to apply a force to it and measure its acceleration.
An astronaut pushes on a spacecraft with a force of 200 N. The spacecraft accelerates at 0.12 m/s^2.
What is the mass of the spacecraft?

f In the space below, draw a falling stone with the following forces acting on it:

- its weight, 8.0 N

- air resistance, 2.4 N.

g Calculate the stone's acceleration. (Its mass is 0.80 kg.)

Exercise P3.5 Mass and weight

Mass and weight are two quantities that can easily be confused.

How well do you understand the difference between mass and weight? In the second column of the table, write 'mass' or 'weight' (or 'both'), as appropriate.

Description	Mass or weight or both?
a force	
measured in kilograms	
measured in newtons	
decreases if you go to the Moon	
a measure of how difficult it is to accelerate a body	
caused by the attraction of another body	
increases if more atoms are added to a body	
balanced by the contact force of the floor when you are standing	
makes it difficult to change the direction of a body as it moves	
decreases to zero as a body moves far from the Earth or any other object	

Exercise P3.6 Falling

What is the pattern of motion of a falling object? How do the forces of gravity and friction affect a falling body?

Galileo is said to have dropped two objects of different masses from the top of the Leaning Tower of Pisa. The diagram shows the position of the smaller object at equal intervals of time as it fell.

a The spacing between the dots gradually increases. What does this tell you about the velocity of the falling object?

....

....

b On the diagram, add dots to show the pattern you would expect to find for the object with greater mass (at the same intervals of time).

c What can you say about the accelerations of the two objects?

....

....

d Galileo's young assistant would probably have enjoyed attaching a parachute to a stone and dropping it from the tower. After a short time, the stone would fall at a constant velocity. On the diagram, add some small crosses to show the pattern you would expect to see for this.

e The graph shows how the stone's speed would change as it fell. On the right are two drawings of the stone. These correspond to points A and B on the graph.

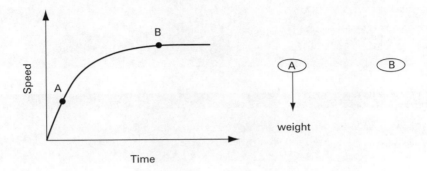

Diagram A shows the stone's weight. Add a second force arrow to this diagram to show the force of air resistance acting on the stone at point A.

Add two force arrows to diagram B to show the forces acting on the stone at this point B in its fall.

Exercise P4.1 Turning effect of a force

> When a force acts on a body that is pivoted, it can have a turning effect. The body may start to rotate.

a   The diagram shows a wheelbarrow with a heavy load of soil. Add an arrow to show how you could lift the left-hand end of the barrow with the smallest force possible. Remember to indicate clearly the direction of the force.

b The diagram shows a beam balanced on a pivot. Add arrows to show the following forces:

  • A 100 N force pressing downwards on the beam that will have the greatest possible clockwise turning effect. Label this force A.

  • A 200 N force pressing downwards on the beam that will have an anticlockwise turning effect equal in size to the turning effect of force A. Label this force B.

c If a body is in equilibrium, what can you say about:

  • the resultant force on the body?

  ....

  • the resultant turning effect on the body?

  ....

Exercise P4.2 Calculating moments

> In this exercise, you will calculate some moments. Remember that it is important to note whether a moment acts in a clockwise or anticlockwise direction.

a In the diagram, all the forces are of equal size.

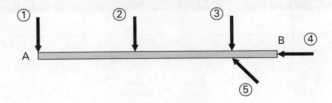

Which force has the greatest moment about point A? ....

Which force has no moment about point B? ....

b Look at the diagram.

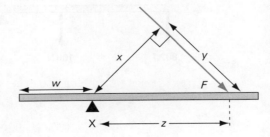

Which distance should be used in calculating the moment of force *F* about point X? ....

Explain why you chose this distance for your answer.

....

....

....

c Calculate the moment about the pivot of each force in the diagram. Write your answers in the table.

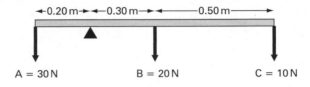

Force	Moment	Clockwise or anticlockwise?
A		
B		
C		

Which force must be removed if the beam is to be balanced? ....

d In the diagram, the beam is balanced (in equilibrium). Calculate the size of force *F*.

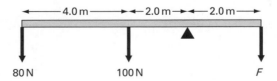

Exercise P4.3 Stability and centre of mass

An object is stable if it will not topple over easily.

a The first diagram shows an object that is fairly stable. Its centre of mass is marked with a dot. This is the point at which the mass of an object can be considered to be concentrated.

On the left of this object, draw an object that is more stable. Mark its centre of mass.

On the right of this object, draw an object that is less stable. Mark its centre of mass.

b The second diagram shows two objects that are not very stable. The centre of mass of each is marked with a dot.

Two vertical forces act on each of these objects. Name them.

upward force: ....

downward force: ....

For each object, draw arrows showing the two forces acting on it. Decide whether each object will fall over. Write an explanation under the diagram.

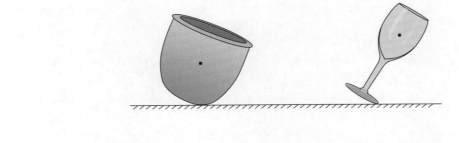

....

....

....

....

....

....

Exercise P4.4 Finding the centre of mass of a thin sheet of card

> In this exercise you will explain how to find the position of the centre of mass of a 'lamina' – a thin sheet of card of uniform thickness.

Here are the initial instructions for this experiment. Read them carefully and answer the questions which follow.

1 Cut a shape from the card. This is your lamina.
2 Use the pin to make three holes around the edge of the lamina.
3 Fix the pin horizontally in the clamp.
4 Using one hole, hang the lamina from the pin. Make sure that it can turn freely.
5 Hang the string from the pin so that the weight makes it hang vertically. Mark two points on the lamina along the length of the string.

a List the equipment and materials needed for this experiment.

....

....

....

....

b The lamina hangs freely from the pin. What can you say about the position of its centre of mass?

....

....

....

....

c Complete the list of instructions to explain how you would find the centre of mass of the lamina.

....

....

....

....

Exercise P4.5 Make a mobile

A hanging mobile is usually decorative. You can make one that will help people to understand a bit of physics.

You will need:

- two different lengths of stiff wire (or thin wooden rod)

- cotton thread

- small objects of different weights

- sticky paper or labels

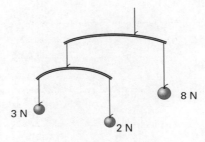

This is what you do:

- Start by weighing your chosen objects. Label them with their approximate weights.

- Take the two lightest objects and hang them from the ends of the shorter piece of wire.

- Attach a piece of thread close to the midpoint of the wire. Adjust its position until the wire balances horizontally.

- Attach the suspension thread to one end of the second piece of wire. Attach the third weight to the other end.

- Attach a piece of thread close to the midpoint of the second wire. Adjust its position until it all balances horizontally.

- Hang your mobile from a high point.

- Write a short script for a talk in which you use your mobile to explain about the moments of forces and how they can be balanced.

....

....

....

....

....

....

....

....

....

....

....

Exercise P5.1 Stretching a spring

Robert Hooke discovered his law of springs by attaching weights and measuring the extension of a spring.

a Add mathematical symbols in the wide spaces to turn the following words into an equation. There are **two** different ways to do it. Can you find both?

stretched length   original length   extension

stretched length   original length   extension

b A student carried out an experiment as shown in the diagram to stretch a spring. The table shows her results. Complete the third column of the table.

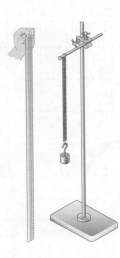

Load / N	Length / cm	Extension / mm
0	25.0	
1.0	25.4	
2.0	25.8	
3.0	26.2	
4.0	26.6	
5.0	27.0	
6.0	27.4	
7.0	27.8	
8.0	28.5	
9.0	29.2	
10.0	29.9	

From the data in the table, estimate the force needed to produce an extension of 1.0 cm.

....

On the graph paper grid, draw a extension–load graph for the spring.

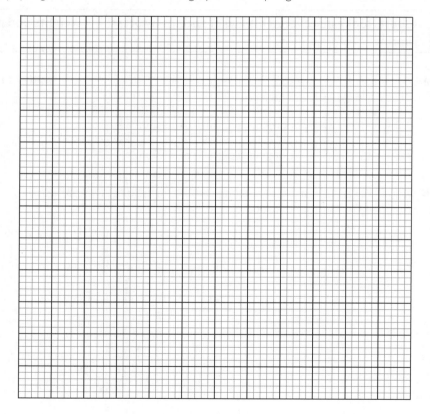

From your graph, estimate the load at the limit of proportionality.

....

Exercise P5.2 Stretching rubber

> **Rubber is an interesting material. It is very elastic (stretchy) and this means that it has many practical uses.**

For this activity, you will need several rubber bands: three identical bands, and another that is broad and long. You will also need a ruler.

a Take one of the three identical bands. Measure its original length. Then stretch it as much as you can and measure its new length.

Record your results here:

....

....

Calculate this quantity:

$$\frac{\text{extension}}{\text{original length}} = \text{.....................}$$

b Take one of the three identical bands. Stretch it by hand. Repeat this with two bands side-by-side, and then with three bands.

The spring constant of a band tells you the force needed to stretch it by 1 cm (or some other standard amount). How does the spring constant depend on the number of bands when you stretch them side-by-side?

....

....

....

c Take the broad, long band. Grip it so that your thumbs are about 2 cm apart.

Touch the band gently against your to lip. This is a good way to sense its temperature.

Now stretch and release the band vigorously about 20 times in about 5 s. Once again, quickly sense its temperature against your lip.

State what you observe, and give an explanation.

....

....

....

....

Exercise P5.3 Pressure

Has an elephant ever stood on your foot? Ideas about pressure explain why it might not hurt quite as much as you might think!

a The equation $p = \dfrac{F}{A}$ is used to calculate pressure.

Complete the table to show the name of each quantity and the SI unit (name and symbol) of each quantity.

Quantity	Symbol	SI unit
	F	
	p	
	A	

Rearrange the equation to make *F* and *A* the subject:

F =   *A* =

b It is dangerous to stand on the icy surface of a frozen pond or lake.

Explain why it is more dangerous to stand on one foot than on both feet.

....

....

....

....

Describe how you could move across the ice in such a way as to minimise the danger of falling through.

....

....

....

c Calculate the pressure when a force of 200 N presses on an area of 0.40 m².

d The pressure inside a car tyre is 250 kPa (250 000 Pa). Calculate the total force exerted on the inner surface of the tyre if its surface area is 0.64 m².

DEFINITIONS TO LEARN

kinetic energy (k.e.): the energy of a moving object

gravitational potential energy (g.p.e.): the energy of an object raised up against the force of gravity

chemical energy: energy stored in chemical substances and which can be released in a chemical reaction

thermal (heat) energy: energy being transferred from a hotter place to a colder place because of the temperature difference between them

strain energy (elastic energy): energy of an object due to its having been stretched or compressed

nuclear energy: energy stored in the nucleus of an atom

efficiency: the fraction of energy that is converted into a useful form

principle of conservation of energy: the total energy of interacting objects is constant provided no net external force acts

USEFUL EQUATIONS

$$\text{efficiency} = \frac{\text{useful energy output}}{\text{energy input}} \times 100\%$$

$$\text{gravitational potential energy} = \text{weight} \times \text{height}$$

$$\text{g.p.e.} = mgh$$

$$\text{kinetic energy} = \frac{1}{2} \times \text{mass} \times \text{speed}^2$$

$$\text{k.e.} = \frac{1}{2}mv^2$$

43

Exercise P6.1 Recognising forms of energy

> In physics, it is important to be able to recognise different forms of energy. Then you will be able to identify energy changes as they happen. In any energy conversion, the principle of conservation of energy states that the total amount of energy before and after the conversion is constant.

a Energy comes in different forms. Sometimes, energy is being stored (chemical energy is an example). Sometimes, energy is being transferred from one object to another or from place to place (for example, light energy).

Complete the table as follows:

- In the second column, name the form of energy described in the first column.

- In the third column, write 'store' or 'transfer', as appropriate.

Description	Form of energy	Store or transfer?
energy as visible radiation		
energy of a stretched spring		
energy spreading out from a hot object		
energy in the nucleus of a uranium atom		
energy of a moving car		
energy in diesel fuel		
energy of a ball held above your head		
energy of a hot cup of coffee		
energy carried by an electric current		

b The diagrams show a rocket being launched into space, and the energy changes that are involved.

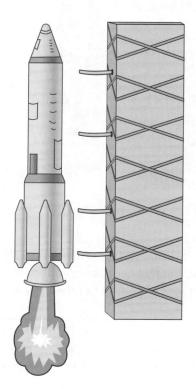

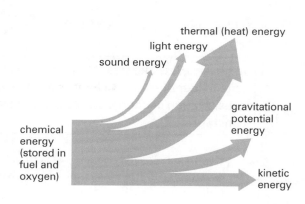

In the table, explain how you know that each of these energy changes is happening. The first one has been done for you.

Energy change: chemical energy to ...	How we can tell
sound energy	The rocket launch is very noisy.
light energy	
thermal (heat) energy	
gravitational potential energy	
kinetic energy	

Explain how the energy flow diagram shows that the principle of conservation of energy is obeyed in these energy changes.

....

....

....

....

45

Exercise P6.2 Energy efficiency

> In many energy transformations, some of the energy is wasted – it ends up in a different form from the one we want. Many energy transformations waste energy as thermal (heat) energy.

a   A washing machine has a motor that turns the drum. In a particular washing machine, the motor is supplied with 1200 J of energy each second. Of this, 900 J of energy is used to turn the drum. The rest is wasted as heat energy.

Calculate the amount of energy wasted as heat each second.

Calculate the efficiency of the motor. Give your answer as a percentage.

Explain why we say that energy is 'wasted' as heat energy.

....

....

b Here is some information about two power stations:

- A gas-fired power station is supplied with 1000 MJ of energy each second and produces 450 MJ of electrical energy.

- A coal-fired power station is supplied with 600 MJ of energy each second and produces 150 MJ of electrical energy.

Calculate the efficiency of each power station.

Which power station is more efficient? ....

c An energy flow diagram can be used to represent energy changes. The diagram here shows the energy changes in a light bulb each second.

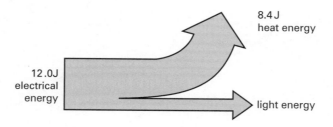

On the diagram, in the correct place, write in the amount of light energy produced each second.

Calculate the efficiency of the bulb.

d In the space, draw an energy flow diagram for the washing machine described in part **a**.

Exercise P6.3   Energy calculations

Because we can calculate quantities of energy, we can make predictions about the outcomes of energy changes. You need to be able to calculate kinetic energy (k.e.) and gravitational potential energy (g.p.e.).

a Calculate the kinetic energy of a car of mass 600 kg travelling at 25 m/s.

b The car in part **a** slows down to a speed of 12 m/s. By how much has its kinetic energy decreased?

c A walker carries a 20 kg pack on his back. He climbs to the top of a mountain 2500 m high. Calculate the gain in gravitational potential energy of the pack.
(Acceleration due to gravity g = 10 m/s².)

d Here is an example of how energy calculations can be used to solve problems.

A girl throws a ball upwards. The ball has a mass of 0.20 kg and it leaves her hand with a speed of 8.0 m/s. How high will it rise?

Step 1: Calculate the k.e. of the ball as it leaves the girl's hand.

Step 2: When the ball reaches its highest point, it no longer has any k.e. – its energy has been transformed to g.p.e.

So now we can write:

g.p.e. at highest point = k.e. at lowest point

$$mgh = \text{k.e.}$$

and rearranging gives:

$$h = \frac{\text{k.e.}}{mg}$$

Use this equation to calculate the height to which the ball rises.

e In a game, a toy car slides down a slope. If the top of the slope is 2.0 m higher than the foot of the slope, how fast will the car be moving when it reaches the foot? (Assume that all of its g.p.e. is transformed to k.e.)

biomass fuel: a material, recently living, used as a fuel

fossil fuel: a material, formed from long-dead material, used as a fuel

renewable: energy resource which, when used, will be replenished naturally

non-renewable: energy resource which, once used, is gone forever

geothermal energy: the energy stored in hot rocks underground

solar cell (photocell): an electrical device that transfers the energy of sunlight directly to electricity, by producing a voltage when light falls on it

solar panel: a device that absorbs sunlight to heat water

nuclear fission: the process by which energy is released by the splitting of a large heavy nucleus into two or more lighter nuclei

nuclear fusion: the process by which energy is released by the joining together of two small light nuclei to form a new heavier nucleus

Exercise P7.1 Renewables and non-renewables

> **Most of the energy we use comes from non-renewable sources. If we used only renewable resources, our way of life would be more sustainable.**

a Complete the table as follows:

- In the second column, write the name of the type of energy resource described in the first column.

- In the third column, indicate whether the resource is renewable or non-renewable.

Description	Energy resource	Renewable or non-renewable?
wood		
natural gas		
coal		
splitting of uranium nuclei		
hydrogen nuclei combine to release energy		
sunlight captured to make electricity		
hot rocks underground used to heat water		
moving air turns a turbine		
water running downhill turns a turbine		

b In the space, draw a diagram (with added labels and notes) to explain why hydro-electric power can be described as renewable.

Exercise P7.2 Wind energy

> The wind can be used to turn a turbine, which turns a generator, which produces electricity. Wind energy is used in almost 100 countries to generate electricity for the grid.

a The graph shows how much electricity was generated from the wind from 1989 to 2010. (The units of energy are TWh, or terawatt-hours. One terawatt is 10^{12} watts.) The table shows the ten countries that contributed most to this total in 2011. (This data is from the Global Wind Energy Council.)

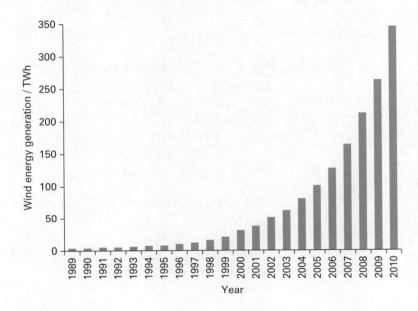

Country	Percentage of world total
USA	26.2
China	19.3
Germany	10.6
Spain	9.2
India	5.4
Canada	4.3
UK	3.4
France	2.7
Italy	2.1
Denmark	2.1
(rest of world)	14.7
World total	100

Study the graph and the table, and then read each of the statements below. Decide whether each statement is TRUE or FALSE. If a statement is FALSE, cross out the incorrect word(s) and write the correct word(s) in the space below.

Here is an example to help you:

The amount of electricity generated from the wind reached 50 TWh in ~~2001~~.

~~TRUE~~/FALSE   2002

i   The amount of electricity generated from the wind has increased every year since 1989.

TRUE / FALSE

ii   The amount of electricity generated from the wind reached 100 TWh in 2006.

TRUE / FALSE

iii   The amount of electricity generated from the wind doubled between 2002 and 2005.

TRUE / FALSE

iv   The top three countries generate more than 50% of the world's wind energy.

TRUE / FALSE

v   The UK makes less use of wind energy than France.

TRUE / FALSE

b   Think of the area where you live. Suggest a good place to put a wind turbine to generate as much electricity as possible. Give reasons for your suggestion.

....

....

....

....

Exercise P7.3 Energy from the Sun

Most of the energy resources we use come originally from the Sun. For example, if we burn wood, we are using plant material that has grown using the energy of sunlight.

a In the table, the first column lists some energy resources. In the second column, indicate with a tick (✔) if the energy of the resource comes originally from the Sun. Indicate with a cross (✗) if it doesn't. The first one has been done for you.

Energy resource	Originally from the Sun?
wood	✓
fossil fuels	
nuclear power	
tidal power	
wind power	
hydro-electric power	
wave energy	
geothermal energy	
sunlight	

b Explain why, when we burn coal, the energy released came originally from the Sun.

....

....

....

....

c Fission and fusion are two processes that release energy when changes happen in the nuclei of atoms. The table lists some features of these processes – but which relate to fission and which to fusion?

In the second column of the table write 'fission' or 'fusion' or 'both', as appropriate.

Feature	Fission, fusion or both?
large nuclei split into two	
two small nuclei join together	
energy is released	
used in a uranium-fuelled power station	
the energy source of the Sun	
helium can be a product	

DEFINITIONS TO LEARN

doing work: work is done when a force moves its point of application in the direction of the force

energy: the capacity to do work

joule (J): the SI unit of work or energy

power: the rate at which work is done or energy is transferred

work done: the amount of energy transferred when one body exerts a force on another; the energy transferred by a force when it moves

watt (W): the SI unit of power; the power when 1 J of work is done in 1 s

USEFUL EQUATIONS

work done = energy transferred

$$W = \Delta E$$

work done = force × distance moved by the force

$$W = F \times d$$

$$\text{power} = \frac{\text{work done}}{\text{time taken}}$$

$$\text{power} = \frac{\text{energy transferred}}{\text{time taken}}$$

$$\text{efficiency} = \frac{\text{useful power output}}{\text{power input}} \times 100\%$$

Exercise P8.1 Forces doing work, transferring energy

> When a force moves, it does work. It transfers energy to the object it is acting on. Use these ideas to answer some questions.

a Complete these sentences:

An apple falls from a tree. The force acting on the apple to make it fall is .... As it falls, its

speed .... This shows that its .... energy is increasing. If its energy

increases by 2.0 J, the work done on it is ....

b The girl in the diagram is raising a heavy load.

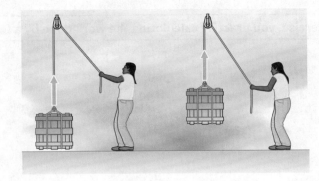

How can you tell that the load's energy is increasing?

....

....

Explain where this energy comes from.

....

....

Explain how the energy is transferred to the load.

....

....

c In the picture, the 20 N force does more work than the 10 N force. State **two** ways that you can tell this.

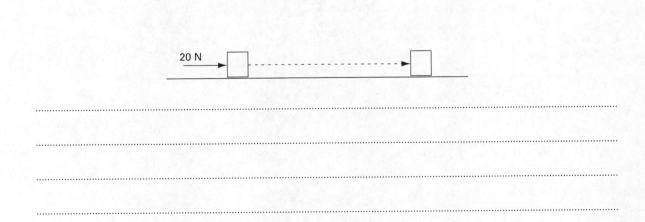

....

....

....

....

Exercise P8.2 Calculating work done

In this exercise, you practise calculating the work done by a force when it moves.

a A boy pushes a heavy box along the ground. His pushing force is 75 N. He pushes it for a distance of 4.0 m.

Calculate the work done by the boy in pushing the box.

b On a building site, a crane lifts a load of bricks. The lifting force is 2500 N and the bricks are raised to a height of 6.0 m. Calculate the work done by the crane in lifting the bricks.

How much energy has been transferred to the bricks by the crane?

....

Name the form of this energy.

....

c The girl in the diagram is lifting a heavy box above her head to place it on a shelf.

- Her lifting force is 120 N.

- She lifts the box to a height of 1.6 m.

Calculate the work done by the girl in lifting the box.

The girl decides it would be easier to push the box up a sloping ramp.

- Her pushing force is 80 N.

- The length of the ramp is 3.0 m.

Calculate the work done by the girl.

59

Give a reason why more work was done pushing the box up the ramp than lifting it straight up.

....

....

....

Exercise P8.3 Measuring work done

> To determine how much work is done by a force, we need to measure the force and the distance it moves.

The student in the diagram is pulling a load up a slope.

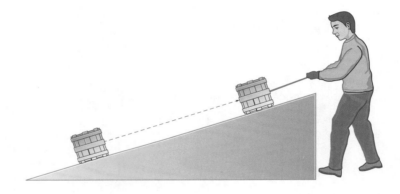

a What instrument could be used to measure the force F that pulls the load?

....

b On the diagram, mark the distance x that must be measured in order to calculate the work done by the force.

c Write the equation used to calculate the work done by the force:

....

d   The student changes the angle of the slope four times. In the space, draw up a suitable table that could be used to record the measurements and to calculate the work done by the force.

Exercise P8.4 Power

> Power is the rate at which a force does work, or the rate at which energy is transferred. In this exercise, you practise calculations involving power.

a   A light bulb is labelled with its power rating: 60 W.

How many joules of energy does it transfer in 1 s? ....

How many joules of energy does it transfer in 1 minute? ....

Why would it be incorrect to say that the bulb supplies 60 J of light energy each second?

....

....

....

b A growing person needs a diet that supplies about 10 MJ of energy per day. Calculate the amount of energy supplied by such a diet each second, and hence the person's average power. (Give your answer to the nearest 10 W.)

c A motor car is travelling at a steady speed of 30 m/s. The engine provides the force needed to oppose the force of air resistance, 1600 N.

In the space, draw a diagram to show the four forces that act on the car.

Calculate the work done by the car each second against the force of air resistance.

What power is supplied by the car's engine? ....

USEFUL EQUATIONS

Boyle's law: pV = constant or $p_1V_1 = p_2V_2$

Exercise P9.1 Changes of state

> Ice, water, steam – these are all the same substance in different states. How well do you know the three different states of matter?

a   Which states of matter are being described here? Complete the table.

Description	State or states
occupies a fixed volume	
evaporates to become a gas	
takes the shape of its container	
has a fixed volume	
may become a liquid when its temperature changes	

b   Label each arrow in the diagram below to show the name of the change of state.

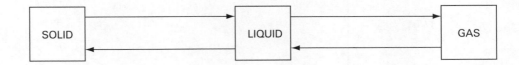

c   Salt solution freezes at a temperature a few degrees below the freezing point of pure water. You have to investigate how the temperature of some salt solution changes as it is cooled from +20 °C to −20 °C. You are provided with an electronic thermometer and a freezer, which is set to give a temperature of −20 °C.

Describe in words and/or with a diagram how you would set about this task.

....

....

....

....

....

....

....

....

On the axes shown, sketch the shape of the temperature–time graph you would expect to obtain. Indicate how you would use the graph to deduce the freezing point of the salt solution.

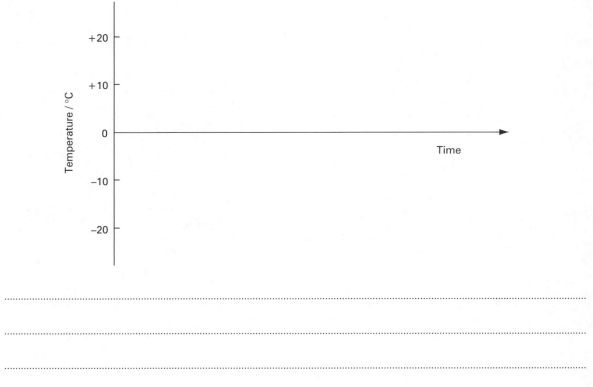

....

....

....

Exercise P9.2 The kinetic model of matter

> The kinetic model describes matter in terms of the microscopic particles of which matter is made and how they move.

a Complete the table by describing the three states of matter in terms of the arrangement of the particles and their movement.

State			
How close are particles to their neighbours?			
How do the particles move?			

b Why is this model of matter described as the 'kinetic' model?

....

....

....

65

Exercise P9.3 Understanding gases

How well do you understand how the kinetic model explains the behaviour of gases?

The drawings represent the particles of a gas inside two containers of the same size. The container on the right (B) has twice as many particles as the one on the left (A), and is at the same temperature.

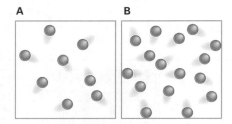

Answer the questions that follow by referring to the diagrams.

a How does diagram A help to explain why a gas exerts pressure on the walls of its container?

....

....

....

b What can you say about the density of the gas in B compared to A?

....

c Why is the pressure of the gas in B greater than that of the gas in A?

....

....

d How could you increase the average speed of the particles in either container?

....

e State **two** changes you could make to A to increase its pressure to be the same as B.

....

....

....

....

Exercise P10.1   Calibrating a thermometer

All scientific instruments need to be calibrated if they are to provide reliable measurements.

A student has an uncalibrated alcohol-in-glass thermometer. She places it in melting ice and then in boiling water. She measures the length of the alcohol column each time. The table shows her results.

Condition	Temperature / °C	Length of alcohol column / cm
melting ice		12.0
boiling water		26.8

a Complete the table by filling in the values of the temperatures.

b Explain what it means to say that the thermometer was 'uncalibrated'.

....

....

....

c You can now draw a calibration graph using the grid below, as follows:

• Mark the two points corresponding to the data in the table.

• Join them with a straight line.

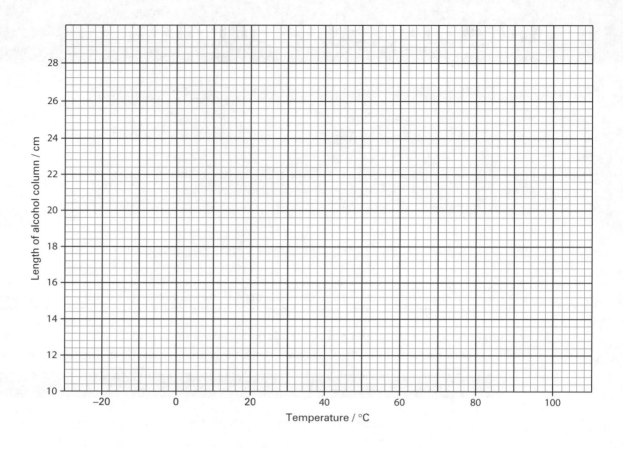

Use your graph to answer these questions (mark the graph to show your method).

i   If the length of the alcohol column is 14.8 cm, what is the temperature? ....

ii   What will be the length of the alcohol column at a temperature of 60 °C? ....

iii The thermometer is placed in a freezer. The length of the alcohol column changes to 10.0 cm. What is the temperature inside the freezer? ....

Exercise P10.2 Practical thermometers

In this exercise you will think about different types of thermometer and what makes them useful for different purposes.

Mercury is used in thermometers because it is liquid between −39 °C and +350 °C. Mercury-in-glass thermometers are used in many different situations. They are attractive for a number of reasons:

a Mercury expands at a steady rate as it is heated. This means that the marks on the scale are evenly spaced. What word describes a thermometer scale with evenly spaced marks?

....

b When the temperature rises, the mercury rises further up inside the glass tube. How could the *tube* be altered to make it rise further for each degree rise in temperature?

....

c How could the bulb of the thermometer be altered to have the same effect?

....

d What word describes a thermometer in which the mercury rises a long way for a small change in temperature?

....

e Explain what is meant by the *range* of a thermometer.

....

....

f State the approximate range of a mercury-in-glass thermometer.

....

g A thermocouple can be used to measure higher temperatures than a mercury-in-glass thermometer. Explain why this is so.

....

....

h Explain why a thermocouple is good for measuring temperatures which vary rapidly.

....

....

....

Exercise P10.3 Demonstrating thermal expansion

It is difficult to see the expansion of a metal even when it is heated by several hundred degrees. The 'bar-and-gauge' experiment is designed to show the effect clearly.

The 'bar-and-gauge' experiment, illustrated in the photographs, is often used to show that a metal expands when heated.

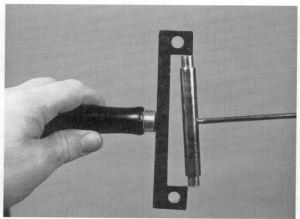

Write a brief script for a teacher who wants to use this demonstration of thermal expansion and who also wants to show that metals contract on cooling. Include practical instructions.

....

....

....

....

....

....

....

....

....

....

....

Exercise P10.4 Thermal expansion

> Most materials expand when they are heated so that their temperature increases.
> Solids generally expand the least, gases the most.

a Give an example of a problem that can arise when a solid expands on a hot day.

....

....

....

b An alcohol-in-glass thermometer is used to measure temperatures in the laboratory. Explain why the liquid moves up the tube when the bulb of the thermometer is placed in boiling water.

....

....

....

Explain why the liquid moves back down the tube when the bulb is removed from the boiling water.

....

....

....

c A bimetallic strip is made of strips of steel and invar, riveted together. Draw such a strip and indicate how it will bend if it is heated. (Steel expands more than invar when it is heated.)

d The table shows the 'volume coefficient of expansivity' for several materials. This quantity tells us the fraction by which the material's volume increases for a 1 °C rise in temperature.

Material	Expansivity per °C (all $\times 10^{-6}$)
air	3400
water	207
gasoline (petrol)	950
iron, carbon steel	33
Pyrex glass	10
invar (a metal alloy)	3.6
copper	51
concrete	36
brass	57
PVC (a polymer)	156

For the materials in the table, answer the following questions:

i Which material expands the most? ....

ii Which material expands the least? ....

iii Which liquid expands the most? ....

iv Which non-metallic solid expands the least? ....

v Why would it not be satisfactory to make a bimetallic strip from copper and brass?

....

....

vi Suggest a better pair of metals from which to make a bimetallic strip.

....

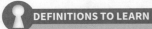
Exercise P11.1 Conductors of heat

Conduction is a mechanism by which heat energy passes through a material without the material itself moving. How well do you understand conduction of heat?

a Copper is an example of a good conductor of heat. What word is the opposite of 'conductor'?

....

Give another example of a good conductor of heat. ....

Give an example of a bad conductor of heat. ....

b The picture shows an experiment used to compare different metals.

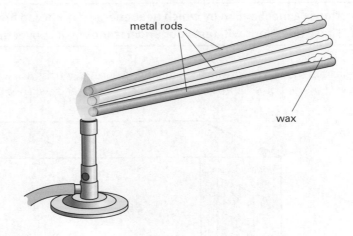

metal rods

wax

State **two** things that must be the same for all three rods if this is to be a fair test.

....

....

Explain how you can tell which metal is the best conductor, and which is the worst.

....

....

....

....

c   Metals are usually good conductors of both heat and electricity. Explain why this is.

....

....

....

....

Exercise P11.2 Convection currents

> Convection is a mechanism by which heat energy can spread around by movement of a gas or
> liquid. These questions will test your understanding of convection.

a   The diagram shows a room with a heater next to one wall, opposite a window. Add to the diagram to show how
a convection current will form in the room when the heater is switched on.

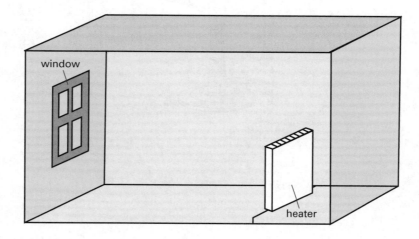

Explain why it would not be sensible to fix the heater high up on the wall, close to the ceiling.

....

....

....

b How do the following quantities change when air is heated? Choose from:

increases   decreases   stays the same

Temperature ....

Mass ....

Density ....

Separation of molecules ....

Speed of molecules ....

c Why does the smoke produced by a candle flame rise upwards? Give a detailed explanation.

....

....

....

....

....

....

Exercise P11.3 Radiation

> **Radiation is a third mechanism by which heat energy can spread around. In this case, it travels in the form of waves, which we call infrared radiation.**

a Explain why energy can reach us from the Sun by radiation but not by conduction or convection.

....

....

....

b Infrared radiation is just one form of which type of radiation?..

Name **one** other form of this radiation..

c Infrared radiation may be absorbed when it reaches the surface of an object. Describe the surface of an object that is a good absorber of infrared radiation.

....

....

What effect does infrared radiation have on an object that absorbs it?

....

....

d In cold countries, windows are often fitted with double glazing. This consists of two sheets of glass separated by a gap a few millimetres wide. There is a vacuum in the gap.

Explain why energy cannot escape from the room by conduction.

....

....

....

Explain why energy cannot escape from the room by convection.

....

....

....

Can energy escape by radiation? Explain your answer.

....

....

....

e A television remote control uses infrared radiation to send instructions to the TV set. If you point it in the wrong direction, the beam misses the TV set and nothing happens.

However, infrared radiation can be reflected by hard, shiny surfaces such as glass or aluminium. In the space below, draw a diagram to show how you could use a remote control, a TV set and a sheet of aluminium to show the reflection of infrared radiation. (You may be able to try this experiment at home. Use a large china plate instead of the metal sheet.)

(Although our eyes cannot see infrared radiation, a digital camera may detect it. Try shining a TV remote control into a digital camera – can you see the camera light up when you press the buttons on the TV remote control?)

Exercise P11.4 Losing heat

There are many experiments you can perform to investigate how energy is lost from a hot object.

The diagram shows an experiment to investigate the loss of energy from a beaker of hot water. Beaker A has a plastic lid; beaker B has no lid.

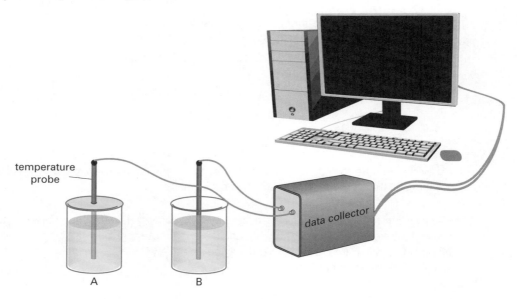

At the start of the experiment, both beakers are filled with hot water from a kettle. The temperature sensors record the changing temperature of the water in each beaker.

a   State **one** quantity that should be the same for each beaker if this is to be a fair test.

   ....

b   State **one** other factor that should be controlled if this is to be a fair test.

   ....

c   Which graph line (1 or 2) is for beaker A? ....

   Explain your answer.

   ....

   ....

d It is suggested that beaker B is losing energy by convection. In what other way could it be losing energy?

....

e Why would it have been a fairer test if the beakers had been insulated around their sides and bases?

....

....

Exercise P11.5 Absorb, emit, reflect

> This exercise looks at how different surfaces absorb, emit and reflect infrared radiation.

In an experiment to investigate how different surfaces absorb infrared radiation, a student takes two metal cans and puts some water in each. She places a thermometer in each can.

One can is painted black. The other has a shiny surface.

She switches on an electrical heater which radiates heat and places the cans on either side of the heater.

a The temperature of the water in each can rises. Explain why this happens.

....

....

b The water in the black can heats up more quickly than the water in the shiny can. Explain why this is so.

....

....

....

c The student has been careful to make her experiment a fair test. State four things in the experimental set up which should be the same for each test.

....

....

....

d The student wants to adapt her experiment to find out which can is a better emitter of infrared radiation. Suggest how she can do this. How will she know which can is the better emitter?

....

....

....

....

....

For each of the sentences below, cross out the incorrect word of each pair.

e A good absorber of infrared radiation is a good/bad emitter of infrared radiation.

f A matt black surface is a good/bad reflector of infrared radiation.

g A shiny surface is a better emitter/reflector of infrared radiation than a matt surface.

USEFUL EQUATIONS

$$frequency = \frac{1}{period}$$

$$f = \frac{1}{T}$$

Exercise P12.1 Sound on the move

> Sound is a way in which energy can travel from place to place. It can be detected by our ears. Check your ideas about the basic ideas of sound.

a What one word describes the movement of a source of sound? ....

Which part of a guitar moves to produce a sound? ....

What moves when a wind instrument such as a trumpet produces a sound? ....

What do we call a reflected sound? ....

b You can probably hear notes of higher pitch than your teacher. How would you show this in the school laboratory?

....

....

....

....

....

c **i** The speed of sound in air is about 330 m/s. How long will it take to travel 1 km? (Give your answer in seconds, to one decimal place.)

ii How far will sound travel in 5 s?

d In an experiment to measure the speed of sound in glass, a pulse of sound is sent into a glass rod, 14.0 m in length. The reflected sound is detected after 5.6 ms (0.0056 s). Calculate the speed of sound in glass.

e The diagram shows a method for determining the speed of sound.

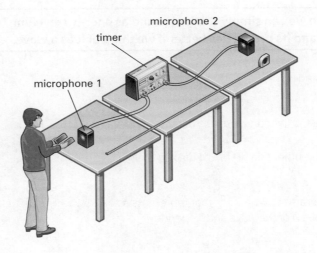

Complete the following sentences:

This experiment measures the speed of sound in ....

To make a sound ....

....

....

....

The microphones detect the sound and the timer shows ....

....

....

....

The boy must also measure ....

....

....

The formula for calculating the speed of sound from this experiment is:

....

....

....

Exercise P12.2 Sound as a wave

> Although we can simply think of sound as energy travelling from place to place, we can understand its properties better if we think of it as a wave.

a Can sound waves travel through a vacuum (empty space)? ....

b What instrument do we use to detect sound waves? ....

What instrument do we use to display them on a screen? ....

c The diagram shows a trace that represents a sound wave. Add labelled arrows to the diagram to show the amplitude *A* of the wave and its period *T*.

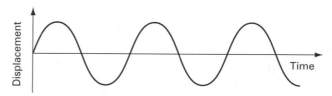

d Humans cannot hear sounds with a frequency greater than 20 kHz.

Write 20 kHz in hertz (Hz).

....

Write 35 000 Hz in kilohertz (kHz).

....

e Arun can hear sounds with frequencies up to 20 kHz. His grandfather cannot hear sounds above 12 kHz.

Which **two** of the following sound frequencies will Arun hear but his grandfather will not?

8.0 kHz   25.2 kHz   16.5 kHz   14.9 kHz   11.8 kHz

....

f A sound wave requires a medium to travel through.

What name is given to a region of a sound wave where the particles of the medium are squashed more closely together than normal? ....

Describe a rarefaction produced when a sound wave travels through air.

....

....

g A drummer strikes the horizontal surface of a drum so that a sound wave travels upwards from the surface of the drum. Describe how a molecule of the air above the drum will move as the sound wave travels upwards. (It may help to include a simple diagram.)

....

....

....

P13:
Light

reflection: the change in direction of a ray of light when it strikes a surface without passing through it

ray diagram: a diagram showing the paths of typical rays of light

real image: an image that can be formed on a screen

virtual image: an image that cannot be formed on a screen; formed when rays of light appear to be spreading out from a point

refraction: the bending of a ray of light on passing from one material to another

refractive index: the property of a material that determines the extent to which it causes rays of light to be refracted

speed of light: the speed at which light travels (usually in a vacuum: 3.0×10^8 m/s)

principal focus: the point at which rays of light parallel to the axis converge after passing through a converging lens

total internal reflection (TIR): when a ray of light strikes the inner surface of a solid material and 100% of the light reflects back inside it

critical angle: the minimum angle of incidence at which total internal reflection occurs

law of reflection: angle of incidence = angle of reflection

law of reflection: $i = r$

$$\text{refractive index, } n = \frac{\text{speed of light in a vacuum}}{\text{speed of light in the material}}$$

$$\text{Snell's law: } n = \frac{\sin i}{\sin r}$$

Exercise P13.1 On reflection

> Ray diagrams are used to predict where an image will be formed. They can be used when light rays are reflected or refracted.

The incomplete ray diagram shows an object in front of a plane mirror. Three light rays are shown leaving the object. Follow the instructions to complete the diagram. Then answer the questions.

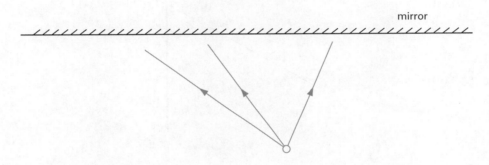

- Extend the rays to the mirror.

- For each ray, use a ruler and protractor to draw the reflected rays.

- Extend the reflected rays to find where they meet.

- Mark the position of the image.

- Measure how far the image is from the mirror.

   a What is the distance of the image from the mirror? ....

   b Is this image real or virtual? ....

   c Explain how you know.

   ....

   ....

   ....

Exercise P13.2 Refraction of light

> **A ray of light is refracted when it passes from one transparent material to another.**

The diagram shows a ray of light travelling from air into glass. Follow the instructions to complete the diagram. Then answer the questions.

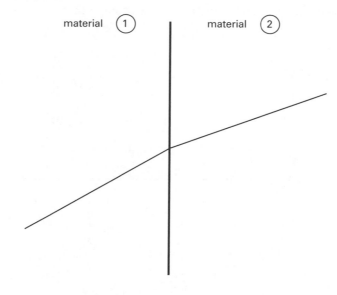

material ①   material ②

- Label the materials 'air' and 'glass'.

- Add arrows to the rays to show the direction in which the light is travelling.

- Using a ruler, draw the normal to the surface at the point where the ray enters the glass.

- Add labels 'incident ray' and 'refracted ray'.

- Using a protractor, measure the angles of incidence and refraction.

a Explain how you know which material is air and which is glass.

....

....

....

b What is the angle of incidence? ....

c What is the angle of refraction? ....

Exercise P13.3 The changing speed of light

Light travels at different speeds in different materials. This is what causes refraction.

a The speed of light in a vacuum is 3.0×10^8 m/s. In water, its speed is 2.25×10^8 m/s. Calculate the refractive index of water.

b A ray of light passing through air enters a block of Perspex. Its angle of incidence is 30°. In the space, draw a diagram of this, showing the angles of incidence and refraction.

The refractive index of Perspex is 1.50. Calculate the angle of refraction. Give your answer to one decimal place.

Exercise P13.4 A perfect mirror

When light is reflected in the process of total internal reflection (TIR), 100% of the light is reflected. Without this, we would not have the internet (which relies on optical fibres). This exercise is about another use of TIR.

a Triangular prisms are often used as perfect mirrors in periscopes, telescopes and binoculars. The first diagram shows how a light ray is reflected by a prism (the angles of the prism are 90°, 45°, 45°).

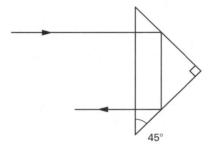

Mark with an X two points at which the light ray undergoes total internal reflection.

What is the angle of incidence of the ray at this point? ....

Explain why the ray does not bend at the point where it enters the prism, or where it leaves the prism.

....

....

....

....

b The second diagram shows a periscope that makes use of two prisms. Complete the diagram by extending the two rays until they reach the observer.

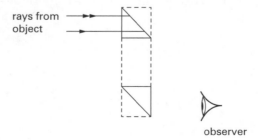

Explain how you can tell from the diagram that the image seen by the observer will be the right way up, rather than inverted.

....

....

....

....

c   The prisms used in the applications shown in parts **a** and **b** are made of glass, whose critical angle is 42°.

State what will happen if a ray of light strikes the inner surface of a prism with an angle of incidence of 30°.

....

What is the angle of incidence of the rays shown in parts **a** and **b**, at the points where they are internally reflected within the glass?

....

Explain why this means that the rays are entirely reflected within the prism.

....

....

Exercise P13.5 Image in a lens

> Converging lenses are everywhere – in cameras, in telescopes, in our eyes. A lens collects rays of light and focuses them to form an image. Check that you understand the rules for drawing ray diagrams.

a   The diagram is an incomplete ray diagram – no rays have been drawn yet! There is an object O to the left of the lens.

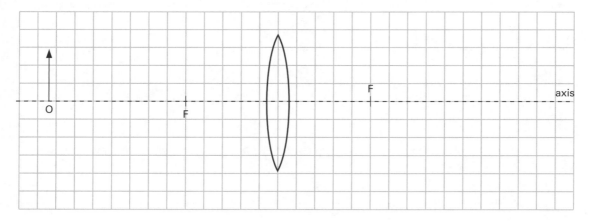

i   What does the letter F indicate? ....

   •   Starting at the top of the object, draw one ray passing through the centre of the lens.

   •   Again starting from the top of the object, draw a second ray that is initially parallel to the axis of the lens.

   •   Indicate where the image of the object is formed.

ii   Which is bigger, the object or the image? ....

iii Which is further from the lens? ....

iv   Is the image upright or inverted? ....

   •   You can use a ray diagram as a scale drawing.

v   If the focal length of the lens is 10.0 cm, how far is the image from the centre of the lens?

vi   If the object is 6.0 mm tall, how big is the image?

b   When a converging lens is used as a magnifying glass, the object O must be closer to the lens than F. Complete
     the ray diagram to show where the image of O will be formed.

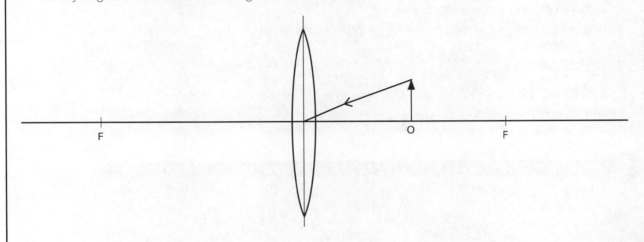

Is the image upright or inverted? ....

Is the image real or virtual? ....

Explain how you can tell from the diagram that the image is magnified.

....

....

....

P14:
Properties of waves

Exercise P14.1 Describing waves

> A wave transfers energy from place to place without any matter being transferred. There are many different types of wave – sound, light, water – but they all have certain things in common. Do you understand the physicists' model of waves?

a The diagram represents a wave.

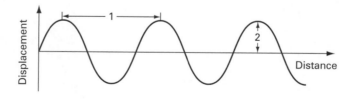

The *y*-axis shows how much the wave is disturbed from its undisturbed level. What does the *x*-axis show?

....

What quantity does the horizontal arrow 1 indicate? ....

What symbol is used for this quantity? ....

What units is it measured in? ....

What quantity does the vertical arrow 2 indicate? ....

What symbol is used for this quantity? ....

b The diagram represents a wave. This graph has the time **t** on the **x**-axis.

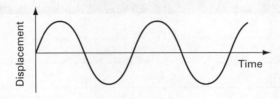

On the graph, add the labels 'crest' and 'trough' in the correct places.

Mark a time interval that represents the period *T* of the wave. Label this *T*.

The period of the wave is 0.002 s. Calculate its frequency *f*. Be sure to give the correct unit.

c Waves can be described as transverse or longitudinal.

In which type of wave are the vibrations at right angles to the direction in which the wave is travelling? ....

Which type of wave is a sound wave? ....

Which type of wave is a light wave? ....

You have a long spring stretched out in front of you on a long table. Another student holds the far end so that it cannot move. How should you move your end of the spring to produce a transverse wave?

....

....

How should you move your end of the spring to produce a longitudinal wave?

....

....

Exercise P14.2 The speed of waves

The speed of a wave is the speed of a wave crest (or trough) as the wave travels along. Wave speed is related to frequency and wavelength by the equation $v = f\lambda$. These questions will test your understanding of this equation.

a Complete the table to show the quantities related by the equation $v = f\lambda$ and their units.

Symbol	Quantity	Unit (name and symbol)
v		
f		
λ		

b A particular sound wave has a frequency of 100 Hz. How many waves pass a point in 1 s?

....

If each wave has a wavelength of 3.3 m, what is the total length of the waves that pass

a point in 1 s? ....

So, what is the speed of the sound wave? ....

c Seismic waves are caused by earthquakes. They travel out from the affected area and can be detected around the world. They have low frequencies (mostly too low to hear) and travel at the speed of sound.

A particular seismic wave is travelling through granite with a speed of 5000 m/s. Its frequency is 8.0 Hz. Calculate its wavelength.

If the wave is detected 12.5 minutes after the earthquake, estimate the distance from the detector to the site of the quake.

Explain why your answer can only be an estimate.

....

....

d Light travels at a speed of 3.0×10^8 m/s. Red light has a wavelength of 7.0×10^{-7} nm. Calculate its frequency.

Infrared radiation travels at the same speed as light, but it has a lower frequency than red light. Is its wavelength greater than or less than that of red light? ....

Exercise P14.3 Wave phenomena

In physics, we use the wave model because it can explain many phenomena connected with light, sound, water waves and many other types of wave. But 400 years ago, few people would have believed that sound, light and water had so much in common.

a Complete the table to show the names of each of these aspects of waves. Hint: each word ends in ...tion.

Description	Name
bouncing off a surface	
changing direction because of a change of speed	
spreading out after passing through a gap	

b The diagram shows light waves travelling through two different materials, 1 and 2.

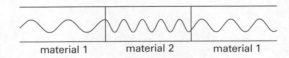

material 1   material 2   material 1

Complete the table to show how the speed, wavelength and frequency of the waves change as they travel from material 1 into material 2.

Quantity	Increases / decreases / stays the same?
wave speed	
wavelength	
frequency	

c   The diagram shows wavefronts passing through a gap.

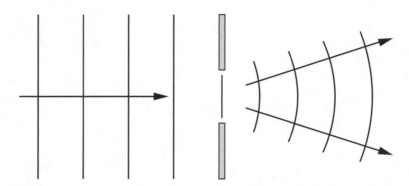

On the diagram, mark the wavelength of the waves.

In the space below, draw a similar diagram to show waves having the *same* wavelength passing through a *wider* gap.

P15: Spectra

Exercise P15.1 Electromagnetic waves

> **Light waves are just one member of the family, or spectrum, of electromagnetic waves.**

a The visible spectrum is the spectrum of all the colours of light that we can see.

Which colour in the visible spectrum has the shortest wavelength? ....

Which colour in the visible spectrum has the highest frequency? ....

Which colour comes between green and indigo? ....

Which colour has a wavelength longer than orange light? ....

b The diagram represents two waves of visible light, observed for a tiny fraction of a second.

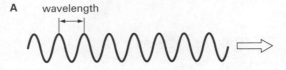

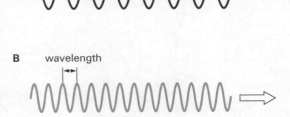

Which wave (A or B) has the greater wavelength? ....

How many complete waves are there in trace A? ....

How many complete waves are there in trace B? ....

99

How can you tell that the waves are travelling at the same speed?

....

....

Which wave represents light of a higher frequency? ....

If the waves represent red and violet light, which one represents red light? ....

c The electromagnetic spectrum is the spectrum of all types of electromagnetic radiation, arranged according to their frequencies.

Which type of electromagnetic radiation has the highest frequency? ....

Which type of electromagnetic radiation has the longest wavelength? ....

Which type of electromagnetic radiation has a frequency just greater than that of visible light? ....

Which type of electromagnetic radiation has the most damaging effects on the human body? ....

Exercise P15.2 Using electromagnetic radiation

Electromagnetic waves have many different uses.

a Below are a list of types of electromagnetic radiation (on the left) and a list of their uses (on the right). But the lists are not in order!

gamma rays
X-rays
ultraviolet
visible light
infrared
microwaves
radio waves

eyesight
transmitting TV programmes
airport baggage scanners
cooking food
sterilising medical equipment
communicating with spacecraft
tanning skin

Draw lines to link each type of electromagnetic radiation with its correct use. (There is just one use for each type of radiation.)

b Electromagnetic radiations have many different uses. For each of the following, write a paragraph describing how the type of radiation is used for the purpose mentioned, and what property it has that makes it suitable for this use. You may have to do some research to find the answers.

i X-rays are used in medical diagnosis.

....

....

....

....

....

....

....

....

ii Infrared is used in remote control devices.

....

....

....

....

iii Microwaves are used to carry mobile phone signals.

....

....

....

....

....

....

> ### DEFINITIONS TO LEARN
>
> **electromagnet:** a coil of wire that, when a current flows in it, becomes a magnet
>
> **solenoid:** a coil of wire that becomes magnetised when a current flows through it
>
> **magnetic field:** the region of space around a magnet or electric current in which a magnet will feel a force
>
> **magnetisation:** causing a piece of material to be magnetised; a material is magnetised when it produces a magnetic field around itself
>
> **demagnetisation:** destroying the magnetisation of a piece of material
>
> **hard:** describes a material that, once magnetised, is difficult to demagnetise
>
> **soft:** describes a material that, once magnetised, can easily be demagnetised

Exercise P16.1 Attraction and repulsion

> These questions will test your understanding of the attractive and repulsive forces between magnets.

a The diagram shows two bar magnets. One pole has been labelled. They are repelling each other.

Label the other three poles in such a way that the magnets will repel each other.

Add force arrows to show the magnetic force on each magnet.

b In the next diagram, the two bar magnets are attracting each other.

Label their four poles and add force arrows appropriately to show the magnetic force on each magnet.

c The diagram shows a horseshoe-shaped permanent magnet attracting a steel rod. The attraction shows that magnetic poles are 'induced' in the rod.

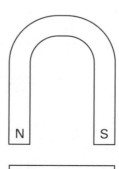

What type of pole (N or S) must be induced in end A of the rod? ....

What type of pole (N or S) must be induced in end B? ....

d If a bar magnet is suspended so that it is free to rotate, it will turn so that its magnetic N pole points towards the Earth's geographical North Pole.

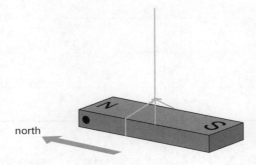

north

What type of magnetic pole (N or S) must there be close to the Earth's North Pole? ....

What type of magnetic pole (N or S) must there be close to the Earth's South Pole? ....

Exercise P16.2 Make a magnet

> **The process of turning a piece of iron or steel into a magnet is called magnetisation. You could try this at home.**

For this activity, you will need a permanent magnet. A fridge magnet is fine.

You will also need a piece of iron or steel to magnetise. A knitting needle or a kitchen skewer may be suitable. You can check by testing that the item is attracted by the magnet.

SAFETY! Take care when working with sharp or pointed objects.

Try to magnetise your iron or steel item by stroking it with the permanent magnet.

After a few strokes, test whether it will attract a paper clip or a staple.

Repeat with a few more strokes (in the same direction). Test again.

Describe a method that you can use to tell if the piece of iron or steel is becoming increasingly magnetised.

....

....

....

....

....

Exercise P16.3 Magnetising, demagnetising

Magnetisation is the process of turning a piece of magnetic material into a magnet.
Demagnetisation is the reverse process.

a   A student strokes a piece of soft iron back and forth using the north pole of a bar magnet. He is surprised to find that the iron does not become magnetised. Where did he go wrong?

....

....

b   A student places a soft iron rod in a coil of wire. He connects the coil to a d.c. supply and switches on. Explain how the current in the coil magnetises the iron.

....

....

c   State one other method of magnetising a piece of iron.

....

d   A student wishes to demagnetise an iron rod. She places it in a coil of wire. What must she then do to demagnetise the iron?

....

....

....

e A student takes two iron rods; one is magnetised, the other is not. He heats both rods. State the effect (if any) that heating will have on each rod.

....

....

f A student is banging two magnets together to feel the force between them. Her teacher asks her to stop as this may damage the magnets. Why?

....

Exercise P16.4 Magnetic fields

> We use magnetic field lines to represent the shape of a magnetic field. From the pattern, we can also tell if two magnets are attracting each other, or repelling.

Complete the four diagrams to show the magnetic field around the single magnet, around each pair of magnets, and around the electromagnet.

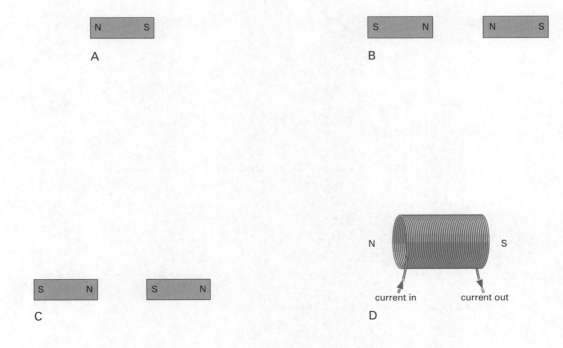

P17:
Static electricity

Exercise P17.1 Attraction and repulsion

These questions will test your understanding of the attractive and repulsive forces between electric charges.

a   A student rubs a plastic rod with a woollen cloth. The rod and cloth both become electrically charged.

What force causes the two materials to become charged? ....

If the cloth has a positive charge, what type of charge does the rod have? ....

If the cloth and rod are brought close to one another, will they attract or repel each other?

....

Explain why this happens.

....

....

....

....

....

b The picture shows one way in which the student could observe the forces exerted by the charged cloth and rod on each other.

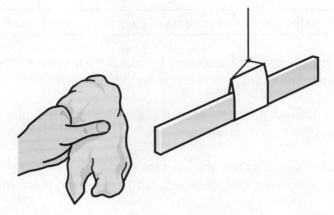

Write a brief description of this experiment – how it is done and what you would expect to observe.

....

....

....

....

....

....

....

....

....

c A student rubs a plastic rod with a woollen cloth. The rod gains a negative electric charge. Before the experiment, the rod had no electric charge.

What one word means 'having no electric charge'? ....

What type of particles have been transferred to the rod? Explain how you know.

....

....

The cloth is left with a positive charge. Which type of particle does it have more of, protons or electrons?

....

Exercise P17.2 Static at home

Investigate the phenomenon of static electricity using some materials you can find at home.

It is easy to generate static electricity by rubbing two materials together. The materials must both be electrical insulators, and they must not be the same material.

Find some different plastic items such as pens, rulers and combs. Find some pieces of cloth made from cotton, polyester, wool and so on.

Rub one plastic item on one of the cloths. Test whether your item has become charged by seeing if it will pick up scraps of paper (use scraps of thin paper less than 5 mm in size).

Try different combinations of plastic items and cloths. Keep a record of your results.

Briefly describe your findings. Was one combination of materials better than another at generating static electricity? How did you make this a fair test?

....

....

....

....

....

....

....

....

....

....

....

....

DEFINITIONS TO LEARN

amp, ampere (A): the SI unit of electric current

cell: a device that provides a voltage in a circuit by means of a chemical reaction

battery: two or more electrical cells connected together in series; the word may also be used to mean a single cell

conductor: a substance that allows an electric current to pass through it

insulator: a substance that does not conduct electricity

current: a flow of electric charge

direct current (d.c.): electric current that flows in the same direction all the time

alternating current (a.c.): electric current that flows first one way, then the other, in a circuit

coulomb (C): the SI unit of electric charge; $1\,C = 1\,A\,s$

ohm (Ω): the SI unit of electrical resistance; $1\,\Omega = 1$ V/A

p.d. (potential difference): another name for the voltage between two points

resistance: a measure of the difficulty of making an electric current flow through a device or a component in a circuit

resistor: a component in a electric circuit whose resistance reduces the current flowing

ohmic resistor: any conductor for which the current in it is directly proportional to the p.d. across it

electromotive force (e.m.f.): the voltage given by the battery that drives the current

volt (V): the SI unit of voltage (p.d. or e.m.f.); 1 V $= 1$ J/C

power: the rate at which work is done or energy is transferred

watt (W): the SI unit of power; 1 W $= 1$ J/s

109

USEFUL EQUATIONS

$$\text{resistance} = \frac{\text{p.d.}}{\text{current}}$$

$$R = \frac{V}{I}$$

$$\text{current} = \frac{\text{charge}}{\text{time}}$$

$$I = \frac{Q}{t}$$

$$\text{power} = \text{current} \times \text{p.d.}$$
$$P = I \times V$$

$$\text{energy transformed} = \text{current} \times \text{p.d.} \times \text{time}$$
$$E = I\,V\,t$$

Exercise P18.1 Current in a circuit

How well do you understand some basic ideas about electric circuits?

a For an electric current to flow, it must have something to flow through. Complete the table by putting a tick (✓) in the correct column to indicate whether the material listed is a conductor or an insulator.

Material	Conductor?	Insulator?
steel		
plastic		
glass		
copper		
silver		
wood		

b The diagram shows a simple circuit.

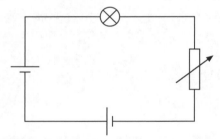

Add a labelled arrow to show the direction of the current in the circuit.

c The circuit shown has two meters. Their symbols are incomplete.

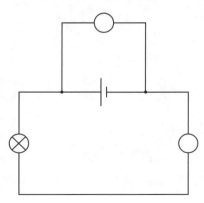

Complete the symbol for the meter that measures the current. Label it with its name.

Complete the symbol for the meter that measures the voltage of the cell. Label it with its name.

d What name is given to two or more cells connected together in a circuit? ....

Exercise P18.2 Voltage in electric circuits

'Voltage' is a term which covers two other terms: potential difference (p.d.) and electromotive force (e.m.f.).

a What is the unit of p.d.?

....

b What instrument is used to determine the p.d. across a component in a circuit?

....

c There are two types of voltmeter which can be used to measure a p.d.: digital and analogue. Which of these gives a direct, numerical reading?

....

How does the other type indicate the p.d. across a component?

....

d Suppose you wish to measure the p.d. across a lamp in an electric circuit. How should the voltmeter be connected in the circuit?

....

The e.m.f. of a cell tells us about the energy it transfers to charges which are pushed around a circuit.

A 1.5 V cell transfers 1.5 J of energy to each coulomb of charge which it drives round a circuit.

e How much energy does a 6.0 V cell transfer to each coulomb of charge which it drives round a circuit?

f How much energy does a 6.0 V cell transfer if it drives 25 C of charge round a circuit?

g Complete the sentence which defines the volt; write the same equation in symbols underneath.

1 volt = 1 joule . . . .

....

Exercise P18.3 Current and charge

> An electric current is a flow of electric charge – the same charge that helps us to explain static electricity.

a When there is a current in a circuit, electrons move through the metal wires.

The diagram shows a simple circuit in which a cell makes a current flow around the circuit. The arrow shows the direction in which the electrons move in the circuit.

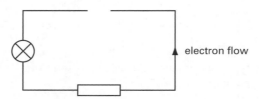

There is a gap in the circuit where the cell should be. Draw in the symbol for the cell, making sure that it is the correct way round.

b The equation $Q = It$ relates current, charge and time. Complete the table to show the meaning of the symbols in this equation and give their units (name and symbol).

Symbol for quantity	Quantity	Unit (name and symbol)
Q		
I		
t		

c Write an equation linking the following units: coulomb, ampere and second.

d If a current of 2.4 A flows in a circuit, how much charge flows past a point in one second?

....

Calculate the charge that flows in 30 s.

....

e An electric motor is supplied with current by a power supply. If 720 C of charge passes through the motor each minute, what current is flowing?

f A battery supplies a current of 1.25 A to a circuit. How long will it take for 75 C of charge to flow round the circuit?

Exercise P18.4 Electrical resistance

> **The resistance of a component tells us how easy (or difficult) it is to make current flow through that component.**

a We say that an ohm (Ω) is a volt (V) per ampere (A). So, if a resistor has a resistance of 10 Ω, it takes 10 V to make a current of 1 A flow through it.

What voltage is needed to make a current of 2 A flow through the same 10 Ω resistor? ....

What voltage is needed to make a current of 1 A flow through a 20 Ω resistor? ....

b The current in a circuit changes as the resistance in the circuit changes. Complete the table by indicating whether the change indicated will cause the current to increase or to decrease.

Change	Current – increase or decrease?
more resistance in the circuit	
less resistance in the circuit	
increase the voltage	
use thinner wires	
use longer wires	

c   There is a current of 4.5 A in a lamp when there is a p.d. of 36 V across it. What is the resistance of the lamp?

d   A student measured the resistance of a resistor. To do this, she set up a circuit in which the resistor was connected to a variable power supply, a voltmeter and an ammeter.

In the space, draw a circuit diagram to represent these components connected together correctly so that the student could measure the current in the resistor and the p.d. across it.

e   The table shows the student's results.

P.d. V/ V	Current I/ A	Resistance R/ Ω
2.0	0.37	5.4
4.1	0.75	
5.9	1.20	
7.9	1.60	

Complete the third column.

Calculate an average value for the resistance R of the resistor.

Exercise P18.5 Electrical energy and power

> **Power has the same meaning in electricity as it had when we were considering forces. It is the rate at which energy is transferred – in this case, by an electric current.**

a   Write down an equation linking power, energy transformed and time.

b   Write down an equation linking power, current and p.d.

c   An electric motor is connected to a 12 V supply. A current of 0.25 A flows through the motor.

Calculate the power of the motor.

d An electrical appliance has a label that indicates its power. The label includes the following data:

110 V   500 W   50 Hz

What is the power rating of the appliance? ....

How much energy does it transform each second? ....

How can you tell that the appliance works with alternating current?

....

Calculate the current that will flow when the appliance is in normal use.

e A lamp has a resistance of 600 Ω.

Calculate the current that flows through the lamp when it is connected to a 240 V mains supply.

Calculate the power of the lamp.

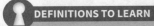

Exercise P19.1 Circuit components and their symbols

> In the previous exercises, you have made use of a few electrical circuit symbols. How many others do you know? What is the function of each component?

a Complete the following table by drawing in the symbol for each component.

lamp	resistor	variable resistor
LDR	thermistor	fuse
switch	cell	bell

b Complete the table by identifying each component described in the first column. (The component names are all in the table in the previous question.)

Description	Component
gives out heat and light	
resistance changes as the temperature changes	
provides the 'push' to make a current flow	
'blows' when the current is too high	
makes a sound when current flows in it	
makes and breaks a circuit	
has less resistance on a sunny day	
adjusted to change the resistance in a circuit	

Exercise P19.2 Resistor combinations

Test your understanding of how current flows in a circuit with more than one resistor.

a Calculate the combined resistance of four 120 Ω resistors connected in series.

b Look at the circuit shown here.

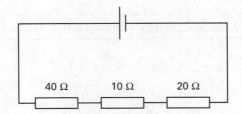

Are the three resistors connected in series or in parallel? ....

Calculate the combined resistance of the three resistors.

What can you say about the current in this circuit?

....

....

c Look at the circuit shown here.

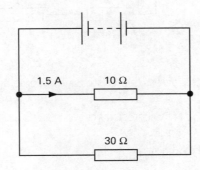

Are the two resistors connected in series or in parallel? ....

One of the following statements is true. Tick (✓) the correct one.

• The combined resistance of the two resistors must be less than 10 Ω. ☐

• The combined resistance of the two resistors must be more than 40 Ω. ☐

The diagram shows that the current in the 10 Ω resistor is 1.5 A.

Calculate the current in the 30 Ω resistor.

Exercise P19.3 More resistor combinations

These questions involve resistors connected in series and in parallel.

a Calculate the combined resistance of four 120 Ω resistors connected in parallel.

b The circuit below shows three resistors connected to a battery.

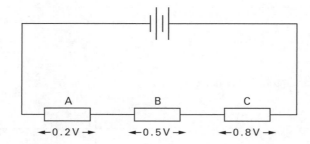

By comparing the p.d.s across the resistors, you should be able to answer this question:

Which resistor has the greatest resistance? ....

Calculate the p.d. of the battery.

A current of 0.15 A flows through resistor A. Calculate the resistance of resistor C.

c   The circuit shows two resistors, A and B, connected in parallel to a 12V battery. The current flowing from the battery and the current through resistor A are marked on the circuit diagram.

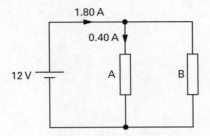

Calculate the resistance of resistor A.

Calculate the current through resistor B.

Calculate the resistance of resistor B.

Calculate the combined (effective) resistance of A and B.

Exercise P19.4 Resistance of a wire

> In this exercise you will think about how the resistance of a wire depends on its dimensions (thickness and cross-sectional area).

The resistance of a wire depends on how thick it is and how long it is. (It also depends on the metal it is made of.)

a Which has greater resistance, a thin wire or a thick wire?

....

Which has greater resistance, a short wire or a long wire?

....

b A copper wire of 30 cm length has a resistance of 0.06 Ω. If it is cut into three equal pieces, what will be the resistance of each?

....

c   A student is given two lengths of steel wire to investigate. Wire A has twice the cross-sectional area of Wire B. She finds that a 100 cm length of Wire A has a resistance of 50 Ω.

What length of Wire A will have a resistance of 120 Ω?

What length of Wire B will have a resistance of 120 Ω?

d   A student has a length of aluminium wire. He measures the p.d. across the wire when there is a current of 0.50 A in it.

p.d. = 4.80 V

Calculate the resistance of the wire.

He cuts the wire into two equal lengths and connects them side-by-side (in parallel). What will be the resistance of this combination?

Exercise P19.5 Electrical safety

> Electricity is useful, but it can also be dangerous. How well do you understand how electricity can be used safely?

a An electric cable may have two or three separate wires inside. Each wire is made of copper or steel and is covered in plastic insulation.

Why is the wire made of steel or copper?

....

....

Why does each wire have insulation of a different colour?

....

....

....

Some cables have to carry large currents. Why are these cables thicker than those that are designed to carry small currents?

....

....

....

b In the space, draw the circuit symbol for a fuse.

An electric heater has a current of 8.0 A in normal use. The fuse fitted in the plug has 'blown' and needs to be replaced. Only the following three fuses are available: 5 A, 10 A and 15 A. For each of these possible values, state whether it would be suitable or unsuitable, and explain your answer each time.

5 A ....

....

....

10 A ....

....

....

30 A ....

....

....

When a fuse 'blows', it must be replaced. What alternative device can be used in a circuit that can be reset each time that it breaks the circuit?

....

DEFINITIONS TO LEARN

electromagnet: a coil of wire that, when a current flows in it, becomes a magnet

commutator: a device used to allow current to flow to and from the coil of a d.c. motor or generator

dynamo effect: electricity is generated when a coil moves near a magnet

a.c. generator: a device, such as a dynamo, used to generate alternating current (a.c.)

national grid: the system of power lines, pylons and transformers used to carry electricity around a country

power lines: cables used to carry electricity from power stations to consumers

slip rings: a device used to allow current to flow to and from the coil of an a.c. motor or generator

transformer: a device used to change the voltage of an a.c. electricity supply

USEFUL EQUATIONS

$$\frac{\text{voltage across primary coil}}{\text{voltage across secondary coil}} = \frac{\text{number of turns on primary coil}}{\text{number of turns on secondary coil}}$$

$$\frac{V_p}{V_s} = \frac{N_p}{N_s}$$

power into primary coil = power out of secondary coil

$$I_p \times V_p = I_s \times V_s$$

Exercise P20.1 Using electromagnetism

> Every electric current has a magnetic field around it. We make use of this effect in a number of devices.

a The apparatus shown in the diagram is used to demonstrate the force on a current-carrying conductor in a magnetic field.

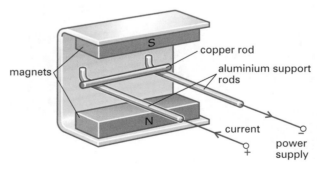

On the diagram, draw a line to show the direction of the magnetic field.

In this arrangement, the force on the copper rod will make it roll towards the power supply. What effect would reversing the direction of the current have?

....

....

....

State **two** ways in which the force on the copper rod could be increased.

....

....

....

....

b An electric motor can be made using a coil of wire that rotates in a magnetic field.

Which part of the motor acts as an electromagnet? ....

Electric current enters and leaves the coil via two brushes. Name the part of the motor against which the brushes press, to transfer the current to the coil. ....

127

Exercise P20.2 Electricity generation

Electromagnetic induction is the process in which a current is induced in a conductor when it moves in a magnetic field.

a Complete the table by indicating whether a current will be induced (made to flow). In each case, assume that the wire is part of a complete circuit. Write 'Yes' or 'No' in the second column.

Case	Current induced?
a wire is moved through the field of a magnet	
a magnet is held close to a wire	
a magnet is moved into a coil of wire	
a magnet is moved out of a coil of wire	
a magnet rests in a coil of wire	

b Alternating current is generated using an a.c. generator. This is similar to an electric motor, working in reverse.

An a.c. generator does not have a commutator. Instead, current enters and leaves the spinning coil through brushes that press on the ....

The diagram shows how an alternating current varies with time. On the diagram, mark one cycle of the alternating current.

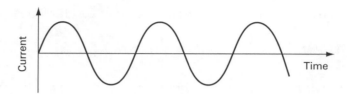

c Fill in the missing words in the following sentences:

In a power station, high-pressure steam from the boilers causes a .... to spin, and this makes the generators turn. The voltage of the electricity coming from the generators is increased using .... The electricity is then distributed to consumers via the power lines of the ....

Exercise P20.3 Transformers

> **Transformers make use of electromagnetic induction to change the voltage and current of an alternating supply.**

a The diagram shows a step-up transformer. In such a transformer, which coil has more turns, the primary or the secondary? ....

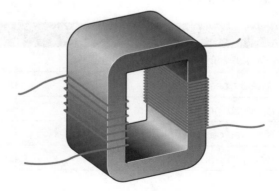

On the diagram, label the **primary coil**, the **secondary coil** and the **iron core**.

b In the circuit diagram, a transformer is being used to change the mains voltage to a lower value so that it will light a 12 V lamp.

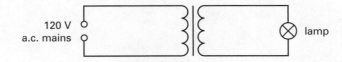

Is this a step-up or step-down transformer? ....

If the primary coil has 1000 turns, how many turns must the secondary have?

c At a small power station, the generator produces alternating current at a voltage of 10 kV. This must be reduced to 415 V for use in a factory.

The transformer used for this purpose has a primary coil of 2000 turns. How many turns must its secondary coil have?

In normal operation, the current from the generator is 4.5 A. What power is being generated?

Calculate the current flowing in the cables in the factory. (Assume that all of the electrical power generated is transmitted to the factory.)

DEFINITIONS TO LEARN

electron: a negatively charged particle, smaller than an atom

proton: a positively charged particle found in the atomic nucleus

proton number (Z): the number of protons in an atomic nucleus

neutron: an electrically neutral particle found in the atomic nucleus

neutron number (N): the number of neutrons in the nucleus of an atom

nucleon: a particle found in the atomic nucleus: a proton or a neutron

nucleon number (A): the number of protons and neutrons in an atomic nucleus

nuclide: a 'species' of nucleus having particular values of proton number and nucleon number

isotope: isotopes of an element have the same proton number but different nucleon numbers

USEFUL EQUATIONS

proton number + neutron number = nucleon number

$$Z + N = A$$

Exercise P21.1 The structure of the atom

> **Everything is made of atoms, but what are atoms made of?**

a The diagram shows a simple model of an atom.

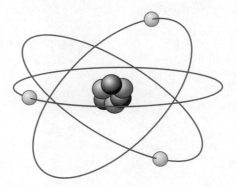

Label the nucleus and an electron.

b Which part of the atom contains most of its mass? ....

Which part of the atom contains all of its positive charge? ....

c   Complete the table by identifying the particles described. Choose from protons, neutrons and electrons.

Description	Which particles?
these particles make up the nucleus	
these particles orbit the nucleus	
these particles have very little mass	
these particles have no electric charge	
these particles have an exactly opposite charge to an electron	

d   The nucleus of a particular atom of carbon (C) is represented like this:

$^{13}_{6}C$

State the value of its proton number Z. ....

State the value of its nucleon number A. ....

Calculate the value of its neutron number N.

e   The nucleus of a particular atom of oxygen (O) is made up of 8 protons and 8 neutrons.

In the space below, write the symbol for this nucleus in the form $^{A}_{Z}O$.

Exercise P21.2 Isotopes

Atoms of an element come in more than one form. These different forms are called isotopes.

a What is the same for two isotopes of an element?

....

What is different for two isotopes of an element?

....

b The diagram represents an atom of an isotope of boron (B).

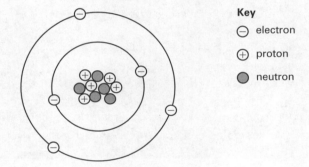

Key
- ⊖ electron
- ⊕ proton
- ⬤ neutron

Write down the symbol for this nuclide in the form $^A_Z X$.

c The table shows some values of Z, N and A for six different nuclides.

Complete the table as follows:

- Fill in the missing values of Z, N and A, in the second, third and fourth columns.

- Use a Periodic Table to identify the elements, and write your answer in the fifth column.

- Finally, in the last column, write the symbol for each nuclide in the form $^A_Z X$.

Nuclide	Proton number Z	Neutron number N	Nucleon number A	Name of element	Nuclide symbol $^A_Z X$
Nu-1	4	5			
Nu-2	5	7			
Nu-3		4	8		
Nu-4	6		11		
Nu-5		6	11		

DEFINITIONS TO LEARN

radioactive substance: a substance that decays by emitting radiation from its atomic nuclei

radiation: energy spreading out from a source carried by particles or waves

background radiation: the radiation from the environment to which we are exposed all the time

contaminated: when an object has acquired some unwanted radioactive substance

irradiated: when an object has been exposed to radiation

penetrating power: how far radiation can penetrate into different materials

radioactive decay: the decay of a radioactive isotope when its atomic nuclei emit radiation

alpha decay: the decay of a radioactive nucleus by emission of an alpha particle

alpha particle (α-particle): a particle of two protons and two neutrons emitted by an atomic nucleus during radioactive decay

beta decay: the decay of a radioactive nucleus by emission of a beta particle

beta particle (β-particle): a particle (an electron) emitted by an atomic nucleus during radioactive decay

gamma ray (γ-ray): electromagnetic radiation emitted by an atomic nucleus during radioactive decay

radioisotope: a radioactive isotope of an element

ionisation: when a particle (atom or molecule) becomes electrically charged by losing or gaining electrons

ionising radiation: radiation, for example from radioactive substances, that causes ionisation

half-life: the average time taken for half the atoms in a sample of a radioactive isotope to decay

Exercise P22.1 The nature of radiation

> Radioactive substances emit radiation. As it passes through a material, it may be absorbed. This helps us to distinguish the three types of radiation.

a The diagram shows how the three types of radiation from radioactive substances are absorbed by different materials.

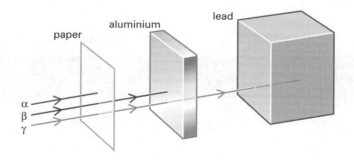

The diagram uses symbols. Write the full names of those symbols here:

α ....

β ....

γ ....

Which type of radiation is the most penetrating? ....

Which type of radiation can be absorbed by a few centimetres of air or by a thin sheet of paper?

....

Which types of radiation are absorbed by a thick sheet of lead? ....

b The radiation from radioactive substances is called 'ionising radiation'. This is because it can damage atoms, causing them to become ions.

What is an ion?

....

....

c Which type of ionising radiation has no mass? ....

Which type of ionising radiation has a positive charge? ....

Which type of ionising radiation is an electron? ....

Which type of ionising radiation is the same as a helium nucleus? ....

Which type of ionising radiation travels at the speed of light? ....

Which type of ionising radiation has a negative charge? ....

Which type of ionising radiation is a form of electromagnetic radiation? ....

d We are continuously exposed to radiation coming from the environment.

What name is given to this radiation? ....

Where do cosmic rays come from? ....

How do radioactive elements in our food contribute to the dose of radiation we receive?

....

How do the rocks around us contribute to the dose of radiation we receive?

....

Exercise P22.2 Radioactive decay equations

> When a radioactive atom decays, it emits a particle from its nucleus. We can use equations to show how the composition of the nucleus changes.

a There are two types of particle that can be emitted during radioactive decay, alpha and beta. The table shows the symbols used for these particles when we write decay equations.

In the last column of the table, state the composition of each of them in terms of the subatomic particles: protons, neutrons and electrons.

Particle	Symbol	Composition
alpha, α	^4_2He	
beta, β	$^0_{-1}\text{e}$	

b The equation shows how an isotope of radium decays to become an isotope of radon.

$$^{223}_{88}\text{Ra} \rightarrow\ ^{219}_{86}\text{Rn} + ^4_2\text{He} + \text{energy}$$

What is the chemical symbol for radium? ....

What is the chemical symbol for radon? ....

What type of particle is emitted? ....

We can check that the equation is balanced by counting the number of nucleons before and after the decay, and the number of protons before and after.

For the nucleons, we have $223 = 219 + 4$

Show that the number of protons is the same before and after the decay.

....

c Which type of radioactive emission does not change the number of protons or neutrons in the nucleus?

....

d In which type of radioactive emission does the number of protons in the nucleus change? Does it increase or decrease?

....

e The equation shows how an isotope of carbon decays to become an isotope of nitrogen.

$$^{15}_{6}C \rightarrow {}^{15}_{7}N + {}^{0}_{-1}e + energy$$

Show that this equation is balanced.

....

....

f Complete the following decay equation, which shows how an isotope of polonium decays to become an isotope of lead.

$$^{211}_{84}Po \rightarrow {}^{207}_{82}Pb + ... + ...$$

g An isotope of protactinium (symbol Pa) has 91 protons and 140 neutrons in its nucleus.

Write the symbol for this nuclide. ....

The nuclide decays by alpha emission to become an isotope of actinium (symbol Ac).

Write a complete decay equation for this decay.

....

Exercise P22.3 Radioactive decay

> The decay of radioactive substances follows a particular pattern, which arises from the random nature of decay.

a A sample of a radioactive substance contains 2400 undecayed atoms.

Calculate the number that will remain after three half-lives.

Calculate the number that will decay during three half-lives.

137

b A sample of a radioactive substance contains 1000 undecayed atoms. Its half-life is 4.5 years.

Calculate the number that will remain undecayed after 9.0 years.

c A radioactive substance has a half-life of 13 years.

Calculate the time it will take for the number of undecayed atoms in a sample to fall to one-eighth of their original number.

d The table shows how the activity of a radioactive sample changed as it decayed.

Time / h	0	2	4	6	8
Activity / counts per second	500	280	160	95	55

On the grid, draw a graph of activity against time and use it to deduce the half-life of the substance.

Show your method on the graph.

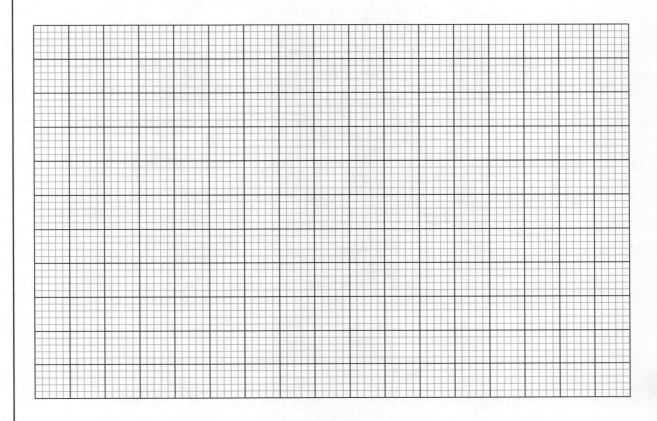

Half-life is approximately ....

e The graph shows the amount of undecayed material in a sample of a radioactive substance as it decayed. When the material had decayed to a very low level, the detector still recorded background radiation.

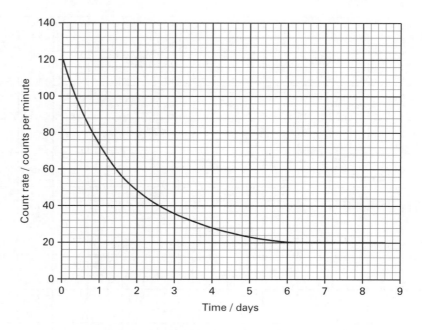

From the graph, determine the background count rate. ....

Determine the initial count rate due to the radioactive substance by calculating:

initial count rate – background count rate

Determine the approximate half-life of the substance.

There are **two** different ways to do this. Can you find both? Show your working on the graph and in the space.

Half-life is approximately ....

Exercise P1.1
The SI system of units

a metre (m)

 cubic metre (m³)

b kilometre (km)

 millimetre (mm)

c 100

 1000

d *For example*: inch, foot, yard, mile, furlong, etc.

e *For example*: to make it easier to compare measurements; to make it easier to share data

f *For example*: medicine (doctors, nurses), engineering, architecture and surveying, etc.

Exercise P1.2
Paper measurements

Answers will depend on the piece of paper selected by the student.

For example, the table should resemble the following:

Measurement	Length / cm	Length² / cm²
short side	12.5	156
long side	17.3	299
diagonal	21.3	454

(short side)² + (long side)² = 156 + 299 = 455

Comments will vary.

Exercise P1.3
Density data

a

Material	State / type	Density / kg/m³	Density / g/cm³
water	liquid / non-metal	1 000	1.000
ethanol	liquid / non-metal	800	0.800
olive oil	liquid / non-metal	920	0.920
mercury	liquid / metal	13 500	13.500
ice	solid / non-metal	920	0.920
diamond	solid / non-metal	3 500	3.500
cork	solid / non-metal	250	0.250
chalk	solid / non-metal	2 700	2.700
iron	solid / metal	7 900	7.900
tungsten	solid / metal	19 300	19.300
aluminium	solid / metal	2 700	2.700
gold	solid / metal	19 300	19.300

b Ice is less dense than water.

c

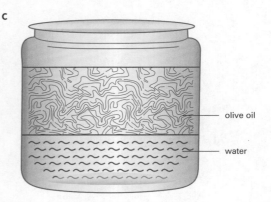

olive oil

water

d Disagree. Aluminium (metal) is less dense than diamond (non-metal). But it is true that, for the table, most metals are more dense than most non-metals.

e 57.9 kg

f 19 300 kg/m³

 possibly tungsten

Exercise P1.4
Density of steel

a   initial level of water; final level of water

b   volume of bolts = final level − initial level

c   bolts completely submerged; no air bubbles

d   a balance

e   bolts are dry/clean; balance is zeroed at start

Exercise P1.5
Testing your body clock

Students should recognise that measuring 50 pulses is better than measuring 10 (provided that the pulse rate is not changing). Also they should appreciate that pulse rate can change, and that this makes it less reliable than using a pendulum.

Exercise P2.1
Measuring speed

a

Quantity	SI unit (name and symbol)	Non-SI units	Measuring instrument
distance	metre (m)	mile, etc.	tape measure, rule
time	second (s)	hour, etc.	clock, stopwatch
speed	metre per second (m/s)	mile per hour, etc.	

b distance travelled

$$\text{speed} = \frac{\text{distance}}{\text{time}}$$

2.8 m/s

c Knowing the distance between the detectors, calculate

$$\frac{\text{distance}}{\text{time}}$$

24 m/s; within the speed limit

0.048 s

d If the time taken by a vehicle is equal to or less than 0.048 s, the warning lights are shown.

Exercise P2.2
Speed calculations

a The green car should be circled as the fastest.

Car	Time taken / s	Speed / m/s
red car	4.2	23.8
green car	3.8	26.3
yellow car	4.7	21.3

b 1 200 000 m

80 min

4800 s

250 m/s

c 10 m/s

15 m/s

It is speeding up (accelerating).

Exercise P2.3
More speed calculations

a 770 m

b 40 s

c 3.60 s

8.0 s

d 2.0 m

The runners speeds might change during the race.

Exercise P2.4
Distance–time graphs

a

Description of motion	Graph(s)
moving at a steady speed	B, D
stationary (not moving)	A
moving fastest	B
changing speed	C

b

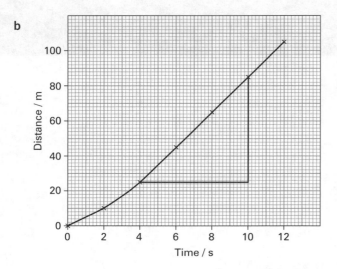

75.0 m

6.5 s

11.5 s

10.0 m/s

c

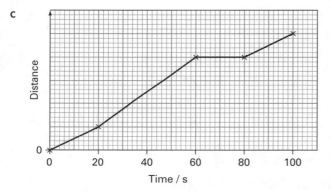

d first section marked as faster

17.5 m/s

10.0 m/s

Exercise P2.5
Acceleration

a its direction of movement

b 8 km/h

c 2.1 m/s²

d 35 m/s

e 6.25 s

Exercise P2.6
Velocity–time graphs

a

Description of motion	Graph(s)
moving at a constant velocity	C
speeding up, then slowing down	A
moving with constant acceleration	D
accelerating to a constant velocity	B

b 1.6 m/s²

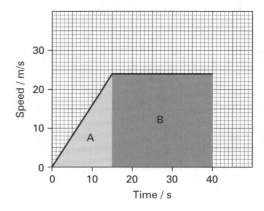

$A = \frac{1}{2} \times 15 \times 24 = 180\,\text{m}$

$B = 25 \times 24 = 600\,\text{m}$

total distance = 780 m

c

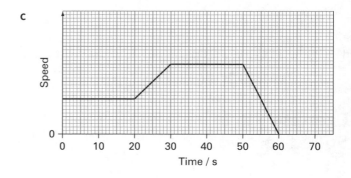

Exercise P3.1
Identifying forces

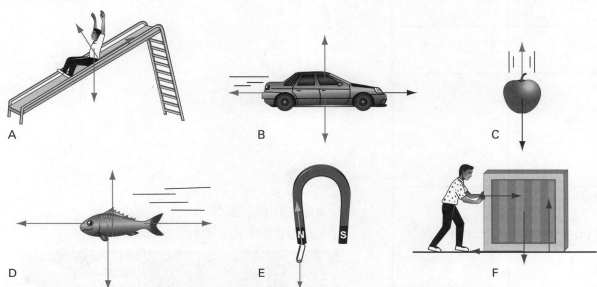

A B C

D E F

Forces and labels should be as follows:

Apple: (up) air resistance of air on apple; (down) gravitational force of Earth on apple

Car: (up) contact force of road on car; (down) gravitational force of Earth on car; (back) air resistance of air on car; (forwards) push of engine on car

Person on slide: (down) gravitational force of Earth on person; (up slope) frictional force of slide on person; (normal to slope) contact force of slide on person

Fish: (down) gravitational force of Earth on fish; (up) upthrust of water on fish; (back) drag of water on fish; (forwards) thrust caused by fish's movements, acting on fish

Paperclip: (down) gravitational force of Earth on clip; (up) magnetic force of magnet on clip

Box: (down) gravitational force of Earth on box; (up) contact force of floor on box; (to right) push of person on box; (to left) frictional force of ground on box

Exercise P3.2
The effects of forces

a A: Van will accelerate / speed up

B: Van will decelerate / slow down

C: Tree will bend over to right

D: Ball will accelerate downwards (but follow a curved path)

b

Friction will make him go slower (*better*: … reduce his acceleration).

Exercise P3.3
Combining forces

a

Forces on object	Resultant force
80 N → □ ← 45 N	35 N → □
60 N → / 50 N ← □ ← 40 N	30N ← □
20 N ↑ / 20 N → □ ← 20 N / ↓ 40 N	□ / ↓ 20 N
20 N ↑ ↑ 40 N / 100 N → □ ← 100 N / ↓ 100 N	□ / ↓ 40 N

b *Diagrams will vary; but must show a body with four forces acting on it with resultant 4 N acting vertically downwards.*

Exercise P3.4
Force, mass and acceleration

a

Quantity	Symbol	SI unit
force	F	newton (N)
mass	m	kilogram (kg)
acceleration	a	metre per second squared (m/s²)

b $m = \dfrac{F}{a}$

$a = \dfrac{F}{m}$

c 14.4 N

d 3.5 m/s²

e 1667 kg (1670 kg)

f

2.4 N

8.0 N

g 7.0 m/s²

Exercise P3.5
Mass and weight

Description	Mass or weight or both?
a force	weight
measured in kilograms	mass
measured in newtons	weight
decreases if you go to the Moon	weight
a measure of how difficult it is to accelerate a body	mass
caused by the attraction of another body	weight
increases if more atoms are added to a body	both
balanced by the contact force of the floor when you are standing	weight
used in calculating the acceleration of a body when a force acts on it	mass
makes it difficult to change the direction of a body as it moves	mass
decreases to zero as a body moves far from the Earth or any other object	weight

146

Exercise P3.6
Falling

a The velocity is increasing.

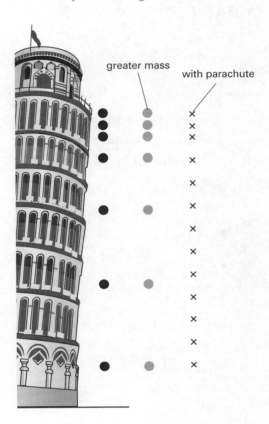

greater mass   with parachute

b See diagram – dots are at same heights.

c The accelerations of the two objects are equal.

d See diagram – crosses quickly become equally spaced.

e

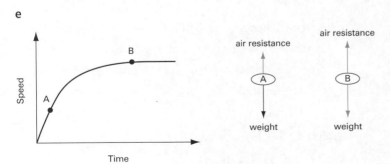

P4:
Turning effects of forces

Exercise P4.1
Turning effect of a force

a force

Note: A vertical force at the end of the handle is a satisfactory answer. Showing the force arrow at 90° to the line joining the handle to the wheel is better.

b

B   A

c resultant force = 0

resultant turning effect = 0

Exercise P4.2
Calculating moments

a Force 3 has the greatest moment about point A.
Force 4 has no moment about point B.

b distance *x*
This is the perpendicular distance from X to the line of the force *F*.

c

Force	Moment / N m	Clockwise or anticlockwise?
A	6.0	anticlockwise
B	6.0	clockwise
C	8.0	clockwise

Force C must be removed if the beam is to be balanced.

d *F* = 340 N

Exercise P4.3
Stability and centre of mass

a

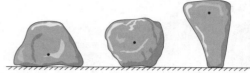

A more stable object has a wider base and lower centre of mass. A less stable object has a narrower base and a higher centre of mass. Typical examples are shown.

b upward force: contact force downward force: weight

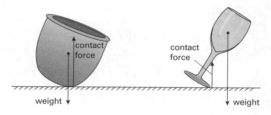

weight   weight

The object on the left will not topple over, as its weight passes through its base and so will cause it to tip to the left, returning it to an upright position. The object on the right will topple over, because its weight is acting outside its base.

Exercise P4.4
Finding the centre of mass of a thin sheet of card

a sheet of card, scissors, pin, clamp, stand, string, weight, pencil, ruler

b The centre of mass is vertically below the pinhole.

c **6** Repeat, hanging the lamina from each of the other holes in turn and marking the line of the string; **7** Use a ruler to draw lines through each pair of points; the centre of mass is where the three lines cross.

Exercise P4.5
Make a mobile

Students should note that, the greater the weight, the closer its thread must be to the point of suspension. When two or more weights are suspended, their weights add together to pull down on the suspending thread.

Exercise P5.1
Stretching a spring

a stretched length − original length = extension

stretched length = original length + extension

b

Load / N	Length / cm	Extension / mm
0	25.0	0
1.0	25.4	4
2.0	25.8	8
3.0	26.2	12
4.0	26.6	16
5.0	27.0	20
6.0	27.4	24
7.0	27.8	28
8.0	28.5	35
9.0	29.2	42
10.0	29.9	49

Force needed to produce an extension of 1 cm: approx. 2.5 N

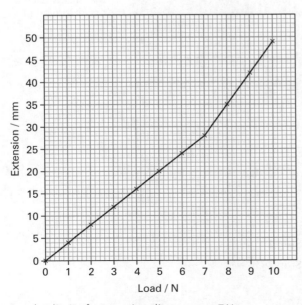

Load at limit of proportionality: approx. 7 N

Exercise P5.2
Stretching rubber

Students' results will depend on their choice of rubber bands.

a Students record original length and stretched length, then calculate extension and $\dfrac{\text{extension}}{\text{original length}}$

b Stiffness is twice as great for two bands side-by-side, i.e. proportional to number of bands.

c The rubber band gets hot; energy has been transferred to it by stretching it. (Work is done on the rubber by stretching it; only some of this is returned when the band is released.)

Exercise P5.3
Pressure

a

Quantity	Symbol	SI unit
force	F	newton (N)
pressure	p	pascal (Pa) or newton per metre squared (N/m^2)
area	A	metre squared (m^2)

$F = pA$

$$A = \frac{F}{p}$$

b Standing on one foot, the downward force (weight) acts on a smaller area, so the pressure is greater and the ice is more likely to break.

Need to spread weight over a larger area, so lie down or crawl, or use an artificial aid such as a plank or ladder.

c 500 Pa

d 160 000 N (or 160 kN)

P6:
Energy transformations and energy transfers

Exercise P6.1
Recognising forms of energy

a

Description	Form of energy	Store or transfer?
energy as visible radiation	light	transfer
energy of a stretched spring	strain	store
energy spreading out from a hot object	heat *or* thermal *or* infrared	transfer
energy in the nucleus of a uranium atom	nuclear	store
energy of a moving car	kinetic	store
energy in diesel fuel	chemical	store
energy of a ball held above your head	gravitational potential	store
energy of a hot cup of coffee	internal	store
energy carried by an electric current	electrical	transfer

b

Energy change: chemical energy to …	How we can tell
sound energy	The rocket launch is very noisy.
light energy	Bright flames emerging from rocket.
thermal (heat) energy	Flames are hot.
gravitational potential energy	The rocket is rising.
kinetic energy	The rocket is speeding up.

In an energy flow diagram, the width of the arrow represents the amount of energy. The width of the initial arrow is equal to the sum of the widths of the arrows it divides into, so the total amount remains constant.

Exercise P6.2
Energy efficiency

a   300 J

75%

The motor is not intended to produce heat.

b   gas-fired station 45%; coal-fired station 25%

The gas-fired power station is more efficient.

c

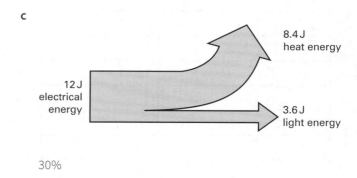

30%

d

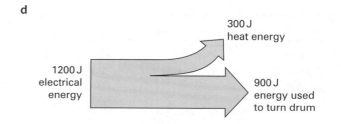

Exercise P6.3
Energy calculations

a   187 500 J

b   144 300 J

c   500 000 J

d   **Step 1**: 6.4 J

   Step 2: 3.2 m

e   6.3 m/s

Exercise P7.1
Renewables and non-renewables

a

Description	Energy resource	Renewable or non-renewable?
wood	biofuel	renewable
natural gas	fossil fuel	non-renewable
coal	fossil fuel	non-renewable
splitting of uranium nuclei	nuclear fission	non-renewable
hydrogen nuclei combine to release energy	nuclear fusion	renewable
sunlight captured to make electricity	solar cell (photocell)	renewable
hot rocks underground used to heat water	geothermal	renewable
moving air turns a turbine	wind power	renewable
water running downhill turns a turbine	hydro-electric power	renewable

b Each student's diagram should show the Sun shining, the water cycle (evaporation, convection, cloud formation, and rainfall on mountains), a dammed river and a hydro-electric power station, with appropriate labels and notes.

Exercise P7.2
Wind energy

a **i** TRUE

ii FALSE; 2005, not 2006

iii TRUE

iv TRUE

v FALSE; more, not less

b Suitable positions are: on a hilltop, in a wide open space, on top of a tall building, on a clifftop. These are places where the wind is likely to be stronger.

Exercise P7.3
Energy from the Sun

a Tick (as originally from Sun): fossil fuels, wind power, hydro-electric power, wave energy, sunlight

Cross (not originally from Sun): nuclear power, tidal power, geothermal energy

b Millions of years ago, plants grew using the energy of sunlight. Plants died, became buried, gradually rotted to become coal.

c

Feature	Fission, fusion or both?
large nuclei split into two	fission
two small nuclei join together	fusion
energy is released	both
used in a uranium-fuelled power station	fission
the energy source of the Sun	fusion
helium can be a product	fusion

Exercise P8.1
Forces doing work, transferring energy

a . . . gravity (its weight) . . . increases . . .
kinetic . . . 2.0 J

b The load is getting higher, so its g.p.e. is increasing.
The girl provides the energy.
The upward pulling force of the rope does work on the load.

c It is a bigger force; and it moves further.

Exercise P8.2
Calculating work done

a 300 J

b 15 000 J
15 000 J
gravitational potential energy (g.p.e.)

c 192 J
240 J
Work must be done against friction on the ramp.

Exercise P8.3
Measuring work done

a A newton-meter (forcemeter, spring balance)

b

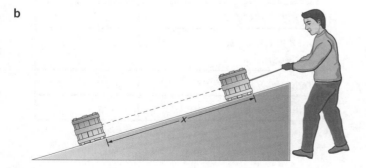

c work done = force × distance moved (in the direction of the force)

d

Angle / degrees	Force / N	Distance moved / m	Work done / J

Exercise P8.4
Power

a 60 J
3600 J
Most of the energy is transferred as heat, not as light.

b 120 W

c

contact force of road

air resistance

forward force of engine

weight

48 kJ
48 kW

Exercise P9.1
Changes of state

a

Description	State or states
occupies a fixed volume	solid, liquid
evaporates to become a gas	liquid
takes the shape of its container	liquid, gas
may become a liquid when its temperature changes	solid, gas

b

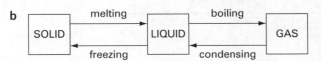

c Put salt solution in a plastic container with space for expansion. Add a temperature probe. Place in freezer with the probe leads out of the door to a data-logger and computer (or temperature display). Record data.

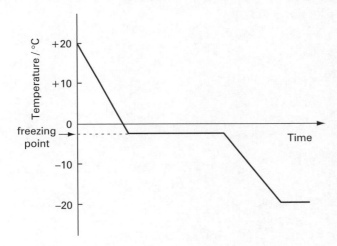

The freezing point is the temperature at which the graph line becomes horizontal. (The later horizontal section indicates the lowest temperature achieved by the freezer, −20 °C.)

Exercise P9.2
The kinetic model of matter

a

State	solid	liquid	gas
How close are particles to their neighbours?	close	close	far apart
How do the particles move?	vibrate about fixed positions	move about within liquid	move rapidly around, bouncing off walls and each other

b   Called 'kinetic' model because particles are moving about, and this helps to explain many phenomena.

Exercise P9.3
Understanding gases

a   Particles bounce off walls; each collision produces a tiny force; many collisions result in pressure on walls.

b   Density in B is twice density in A.

c   Twice as many particles collide with walls each second, so twice the pressure.

d   Increase their temperature.

e   Increase its temperature; halve its volume.

P10:
Thermal properties of matter

Exercise P10.1
Calibrating a thermometer

a

Condition	Temperature / °C	Length of alcohol column / cm
melting ice	0.0	12.0
boiling water	100.0	26.8

b An uncalibrated thermometer has no numbered scale.

c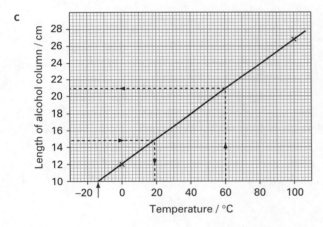

i 19 °C

ii 20.9 cm

iii −14 °C

Exercise P10.2
Practical thermometers

a linear

b Make the tube narrower.

c Make the bulb bigger so that it holds more mercury.

d sensitive

e the lowest and highest temperatures it can measure

f −39 °C to +350 °C

g It is made of metals which melt at temperatures higher than +350 °C

h The junction of the thermocouple (which measures the temperature) is small and so it heats up and cools down rapidly.

Exercise P10.3
Demonstrating thermal expansion

Show that bar fits in gauge while cold.

Heat the bar.

Show that it no longer fits in gauge.

Point out that the expansion is very small even for a temperature rise of several hundred degrees.

Allow to cool.

Show that bar fits in gauge again when cool.

Exercise P10.4
Thermal expansion

a   for example, bridge expanding; railway rails buckling

b   Two-part, straight horizontal bar with upper layer labelled
stell, lower labelled invar.
Then same bar but curved with ends downwards, labelled
as before. (Steel expands more than invar.)

c   steel on outside of curve when heated

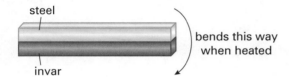

d i   air
invar
gasoline
PVC

ii   Copper and brass have very similar expansivities
so the strip will bend very little.

iii   Invar and copper; or invar and brass

Exercise P11.1
Conductors of heat

a insulator
For example, brass, gold, diamond
For example, air, water, ice, plastics

b thickness, length
Best conductor is the one where the wax melts first. Worst conductor is the one where the wax melts last

c conduction of heat in metals is mostly by conduction electrons and these are also what is required to conduct electricity.

Exercise P11.2
Convection currents

a

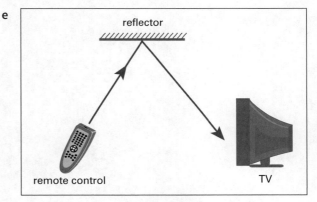

If the heater was high up on the wall, close to the ceiling, the convection current would remain close to the ceiling, and heat would not be distributed lower down in the room.

b increases
stays the same
decreases
increases
increases

c The flame heats the air. The air becomes less dense, and floats upwards. It is replaced by colder air, which is then heated and rises. Smoke is solid particles floating in air, and is carried upwards by the rising air.

Exercise P11.3
Radiation

a Radiation can travel through the vacuum of space. Conduction and convection require a material to travel through.

b electromagnetic radiation
For example: visible light, ultraviolet, etc.

c matt black
Temperature rises and internal energy increases.

d There is no material through which heat can conduct. There is no material that can move as a convection current. Yes, energy can escape by radiation, because radiation can pass through a vacuum.

e

reflector

remote control

TV

plan of room

Exercise P11.4
Losing heat

a mass of water

b external temperature

c Graph line 1 is for beaker A.
With a lid, it cools more slowly.

d Beaker B could also be losing energy by evaporation.

e Insulation of sides and base would mean that almost all heat was being lost through top, which is the area of interest.

Exercise P11.5
Absorb, emit, reflect

a   The cans absorb radiation; this energy increases the temperature of the water.

b   The black surface absorbs more of the radiation than the shiny can. (The shiny can reflects more.)

c   cans same size, same volume of water, same starting temperature, same distance from heater

d   (Remove heater.) Fill cans with hot water. Record rate at which temperatures fall. The can which cools faster is the better emitter.

e   good/~~bad~~

f   ~~good~~/bad

g   ~~emitter~~/reflector

Exercise P12.1
Sound on the move

a vibrating

strings (and body, and air inside)

air (air column)

an echo

b Use a signal generator and loudspeaker (or other source of high-frequency sounds), change the frequency, and ask who can hear each sound.

c **i** 3.0 s

  ii 1650 m

d 5000 m/s

e **i** . . . air.

  ii . . . the student bangs two wooden blocks together.

  iii . . . the time interval between the sound being detected by the two microphones.

  iv . . . the distance between the microphones.

  $$speed = \frac{distance}{time}$$

Exercise P12.2
Sound as a wave

a no

b microphone

oscilloscope

c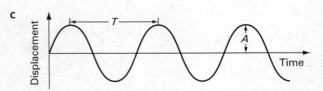

d 20 000 Hz

35 kHz

e 14.9 kHz, 16.5 kHz

f compression; the particles of the air are further apart than normal

g The molecule moves up and down, oscillating about its mean position.

Exercise P13.1
On reflection

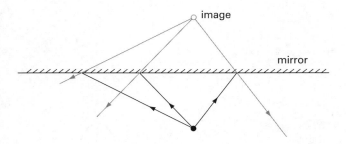

a 3.0 cm

b virtual

c Light does not pass through the mirror. It appears to come
from behind the mirror.

Exercise P13.2
Refraction of light

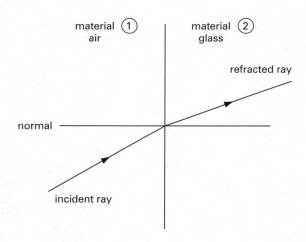

a The ray bends towards the normal as it enters glass.
The angle in glass is smaller.

b 30°

c 20°

Exercise P13.3
The changing speed of light

a 1.33

b

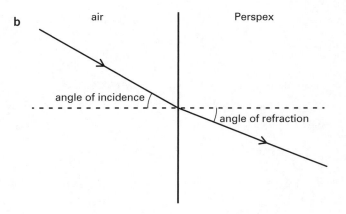

19.5°

Exercise P13.4
A perfect mirror

a

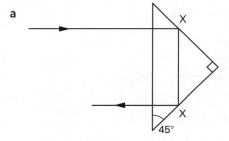

45°

Ray is at 90° to surface, so it does not bend
(angle of incidence = 0°).

b

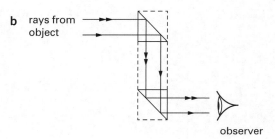

The upper ray (from the top of the object) is above
the lower ray after two reflections.

c The ray will be refracted out of the glass with an angle of
refraction greater than 30°; 45°; the angle of incidence is
greater than the critical angle, so total internal reflection
occurs.

Exercise P13.5
Image in a lens

a i principal focus (focal point)

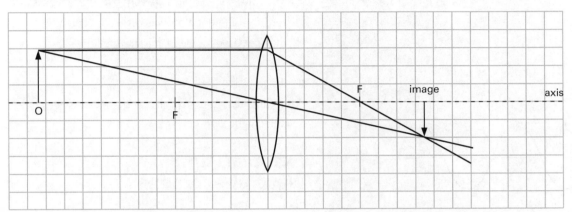

ii Image is smaller than object.

iii Object is further from lens.

iv inverted

v 17 cm

vi 4 mm

b

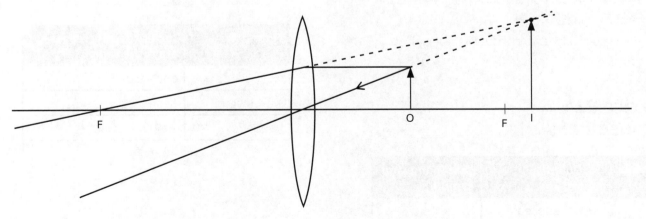

upright

virtual

Image is magnified because it is bigger/taller than
the object.

Exercise P14.1
Describing waves

a distance travelled by the wave

wavelength

λ

metre (m)

amplitude

A

b

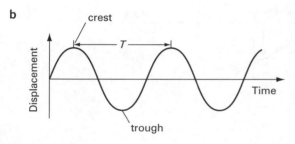

See diagram.

500 Hz

c transverse

longitudinal

transverse

Move your hand from side to side, at right angles to the length of the spring.

Move your hand back and forth, along the length of the spring.

Exercise P14.2
The speed of waves

a

Symbol	Quantity	Unit (name and symbol)
v	wave speed	metre per second (m/s)
f	frequency	hertz (Hz)
λ	wavelength	metre (m)

b 100 waves

330 m

330 m/s

c 625 m

3750 km

The wave speed may have varied as the wave passed through different materials within the Earth. The wave may not have travelled in a straight line.

d 4.3×10^{14} Hz

Infrared wavelength is greater than wavelength of red light.

Exercise P14.3
Wave phenomena

a

Description	Name
bouncing off a surface	reflection
changing direction because of a change of speed	refraction
spreading out after passing through a gap	diffraction

b

Quantity	Increases / decreases / stays the same?
wave speed	decreases
wavelength	decreases
frequency	stays the same

c

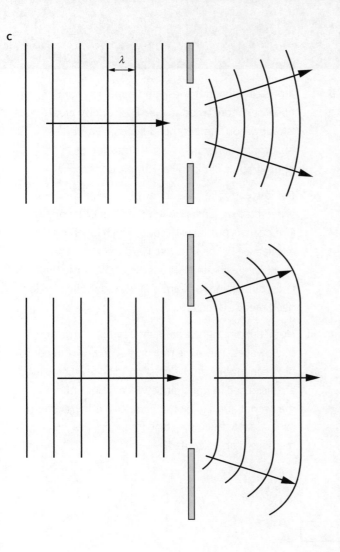

Exercise P15.1
Electromagnetic waves

a violet
violet
blue
red

b wave A
8
14
The waves have equal lengths in the same time.
wave B
wave A

c gamma rays
radio waves
ultraviolet
gamma rays

b i X-rays can penetrate flesh and bone. They are absorbed more by bone than flesh and so create 'shadows' on film or other detectors. Properties: absorption and transmission; detection by photographic film or by electronic detector.

ii Remote control device sends beam of infrared, which is detected by sensor on front of TV or other appliance. The beam is pulsed with code, which identifies the appliance (TV, recorder, etc.) and gives instruction (e.g. change channel). Properties: travel in straight lines; diffract into a beam from the controller, so do not need precise direction.

iii Mobile phone signals are digital signals carried by microwaves. These are transmitted in both directions between mobile phone mast and phone. Microwaves are also used to transmit between mobile phone masts that are in line of sight of each other. Properties: can pass into buildings; high frequency means many messages can be carried.

Exercise P15.2
Using electromagnetic radiation

a
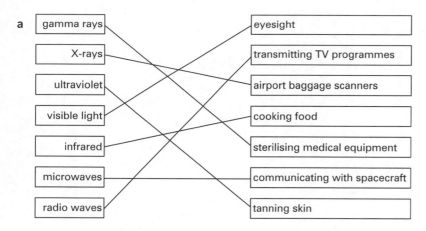

Exercise P16.1
Attraction and repulsion

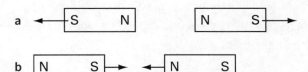

a

b (all the poles could be reversed)

c end A: S
    end B: N

d North Pole: S
    South Pole: N

Exercise P16.2
Make a magnet

For this activity, students should be able to find suitable materials at home. Alternatively, you could lend each student a permanent magnet.

They should describe a valid method for testing the strength of their magnet. For example, at what distance will the magnet start to attract a pin lying on a table?

Exercise P16.3
Magnetising, demagnetising

a The iron should be stroked in one direction only. Reversing the direction undoes the effect.

b The current produces a magnetic field inside the coil and this magnetises the iron.

c Place the iron in a magnetic field and hammer it.

d Connect to an a.c. supply; gradually reduce the current from a high value to zero.

e Magnetised rod is demagnetised; the unmagnetised rod remains unmagnetised.

f Hammering/banging causes demagnetisation.

Exercise P16.4
Magnetic fields

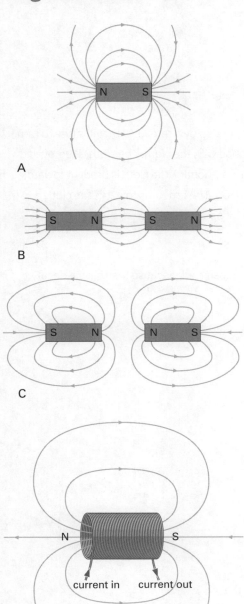

Exercise P17.1
Attraction and repulsion

a   friction

    negative

    attract

    Opposite charges attract.

b   The rod is suspended by a thread so that it is free to turn. The rod is rubbed with the cloth. The cloth is removed. When the rod is stationary, the cloth is brought towards one end of the rod. The rod turns towards the cloth due to the attraction of opposite charges.

c   neutral

    Electrons are transferred, because they have a negative charge.

    protons

Exercise P17.2
Static at home

Students should find that some plastic materials charge up more readily than others, and that some types of cloth are better than others.

They should describe testing this using very small scraps of paper. How close to the scraps do they have to get before attraction occurs? Use a standard rubbing method.

Exercise P18.1
Current in a circuit

a

Material	Conductor?	Insulator?
steel	✓	
plastic		✓
glass		✓
copper	✓	
silver	✓	
wood		✓

b
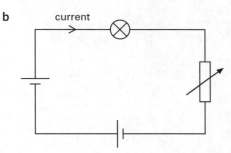

c
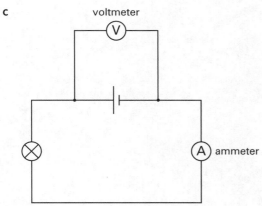

d battery

Exercise P18.2
Voltage in electric circuits

a volt (V)

b voltmeter

c digital; analogue has needle and scale

d in parallel

e 6.0 J

f 150 J

g 1 volt = 1 joule per coulomb; 1 V = 1 J/C

Exercise P18.3
Current and charge

a
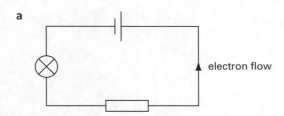

b

Symbol for quantity	Quantity	Unit (name and symbol)
Q	charge	coulomb (C)
I	current	ampere (A)
t	time	second (s)

c 1 ampere = 1 coulomb/second (or equivalent)

d 2.4 C

  72 C

e 12.0 A

f 60 s

Exercise P18.4
Electrical resistance

a 20V
    20V

b

Change	Current – increase or decrease?
more resistance in the circuit	decrease
less resistance in the circuit	increase
increase the voltage	increase
use thinner wires	decrease
use longer wires	decrease

c 8.0 Ω

d

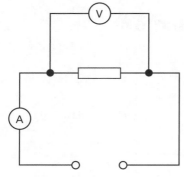

power supply

e

P.d. V/V	Current I/A	Resistance R/Ω
2.0	0.37	5.4
4.1	0.75	5.5
5.9	1.20	4.9
7.9	1.60	4.9

$R = 5.2 \,Ω$

f 0.22 A

g 7.7 V

h Sketch should show I–V graph as a straight line through the origin

Exercise P18.5
Electrical energy and power

a power = $\dfrac{\text{energy transformed}}{\text{time}}$

b power = current × p.d.

c 3.0 W

d 500 W
    500 J
    50 Hz indicates frequency of a.c.
    4.5 A

e **i**   0.40 A

    ii   96 W

Exercise P19.1
Circuit components and their symbols

a

lamp	resistor	switch
LDR	thermistor	fuse
diode	cell	transformer

b

Description	Component
gives out heat and light	lamp
resistance changes as the temperature changes	thermistor
provides the 'push' to make a current flow	cell
'blows' when the current is too high	fuse
allows current to flow one way only	diode
makes and breaks a circuit	switch
has less resistance on a sunny day	LDR
used to change the voltage of alternating current	transformer

Exercise P19.2
Resistor combinations

a $480\,\Omega$

b in series

$70\,\Omega$

The current is the same all the way round the circuit.

c in parallel

The combined resistance of the two resistors must be less than $10\,\Omega$. ✓

$0.50\,A$

Exercise P19.3
More resistor combinations

a $30\,\Omega$

b Resistor C has the greatest resistance.

$1.5\,V$

$5.3\,\Omega$

c $30\,\Omega$

$1.4\,A$

$8.6\,\Omega$

$6.7\,\Omega$

Exercise P19.4
Resistance of a wire

a thin; long

b $0.02\,\Omega$

c $240\,cm$; $120\,cm$

d $9.60\,\Omega$; $2.40\,\Omega$

Exercise P19.5
Electrical safety

a Steel and copper are good conductors.

To avoid confusing the wires; so they are easily identified. Current causes heating. Thicker wires have less resistance, so there is less heating with large currents.

b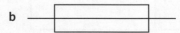

$5\,A$ too small

It would burn out in normal use.

$10\,A$ good choice

It is just above the normal operating current.

$30\,A$ too big

It would not blow with a dangerously high current.

circuit breaker / trip switch

Exercise P20.1
Using electromagnetism

a

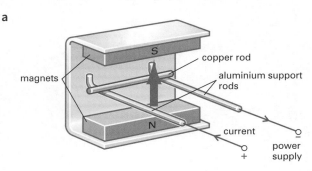

Reversing the current reverses the force, so that it becomes horizontal, away from the power supply. The copper rod will roll away from the power supply.

increase the current; use stronger magnetic field

b   Coil

commutator

Exercise P20.2
Electricity generation

a

Case	Current induced?
a wire is moved through the field of a magnet	Yes
a magnet is held close to a wire	No
a magnet is moved into a coil of wire	Yes
a magnet is moved out of a coil of wire	Yes
a magnet rests in a coil of wire	No

b   slip rings

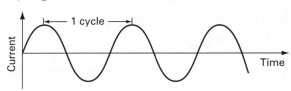

c   … turbine … transformers … national grid

Exercise P20.3
Transformers

a   secondary

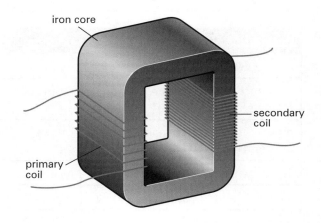

b   step-down

100 turns

c   83 turns

45 kW (45 000 W)

108 A

Exercise P21.1
The structure of the atom

a

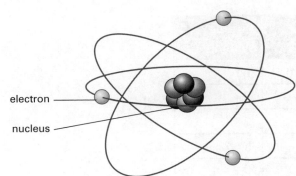

electron

nucleus

b nucleus

nucleus

c

Description	Which particles?
these particles make up the nucleus	protons + neutrons
these particles orbit the nucleus	electrons
these particles have very little mass	electrons
these particles have no electric charge	neutrons
these particles have an exactly opposite charge to an electron	protons

d $Z = 6; A = 13; N = 7$

e $^{16}_{8}O$

171

Exercise 21.2
Isotopes

a number of protons in nucleus (proton number)
number of neutrons (neutron number)

b $^{10}_{5}B$

c

Nuclide	Proton number Z	Neutron number N	Nucleon number A	Name of element	Nuclide symbol $^{A}_{Z}X$
Nu-1	4	5	9	beryllium	$^{9}_{4}Be$
Nu-2	5	7	12	boron	$^{12}_{5}B$
Nu-3	4	4	8	beryllium	$^{8}_{4}Be$
Nu-4	6	5	11	carbon	$^{11}_{6}C$
Nu-5	5	6	11	boron	$^{11}_{5}B$

Exercise P22.1
The nature of radiation

a alpha
   beta
   gamma
   gamma
   alpha
   alpha, beta and gamma

b An ion is a particle that has become charged because it has gained or lost one or more electrons.

c gamma
   alpha
   beta
   alpha
   gamma
   beta
   gamma

d background radiation; space; as they decay, they emit radiation inside us; most rocks contain radioactive elements which decay gradually, emitting radiation

Exercise P22.2
Radioactive decay equations

a

Particle	Symbol	Composition
alpha, α	$^4_2$He	2 protons + 2 neutrons
beta, β	$^0_{-1}$e	1 electron

b Ra
   Rn
   alpha
   protons: $88 = 86 + 2$

c gamma emission

d beta emission number of protons increases

e nucleons: $15 = 15 + 0$
   protons: $6 = 7 - 1$ or $6 = 7 + (-1)$

f $^{211}_{84}$Po $\rightarrow$ $^{207}_{82}$Pb + $^4_2$He + energy

g $^{231}_{140}$Pa
   $^{231}_{140}$Pa $\rightarrow$ $^{227}_{138}$Ac + $^4_2$He + energy

Exercise P22.3
Radioactive decay

a 300
   2100

b 250

c 39 years

d
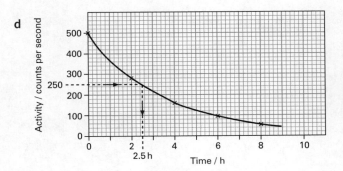

Half-life is approximately 2.5 h.

e 20 counts per minute

100 counts per minute
You can use the pattern of numbers, 100–50–25–12–6–3–1, showing 6 half-lives in about 7 days, or the graph.

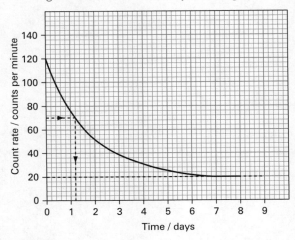

Half-life is approximately 1.2 days.